Chanakya Neeti

Chanakya

GRAPEVINE INDIA

Grapevine India Publishers Pvt. Ltd.
A-208, Second Floor,
New Moti Nagar,
New Delhi - 110015
India

grapevineindiapublishers@gmail.com

contact@grapevineindia.com

First published by M/S Grapevine India Publishers India Ltd.

Printed and bound in India by Nutech Print Services - India

Disclaimer

This is a work of fiction. All characters, organizations and situations are of author's imagination and any resemblance to any person, organization or situation is purely co-incidental.

The author respects all individuals, organizations & communities and there is no intention in this novel to hurt any individual, organization or community.

Contents

Introduction

Chanakya was known by multiple names like Kautilya and Vishnugupta and played multiple roles like being a teacher, philosopher, economist, jurist and royal advisor. He is considered the pioneer of the field of political science and economics in India, and his work is thought of as an important precursor to classical economics.

Chanakya assisted the first Mauryan emperor Chandragupta in his rise to power. He is widely credited for having played an important role in the establishment of the Maurya Empire. Chanakya served as the chief advisor to both emperors Chandragupta and his son Bindusara.

Arthashastra and Chankaya Neeti were the two important books written by him. Arthashastra was discovered in 1905 by librarian Rudrapatna Shamasastry in an uncatalogued group of ancient palm-leaf manuscripts donated by an unknown pandit to the Oriental Research Institute Mysore.

The Arthashastra discusses monetary and fiscal policies, welfare, international relations, and war strategies in detail. The text also outlines the duties of a ruler. Some scholars believe that

Arthashastra is actually a compilation of a number of earlier texts written by various authors, and Chanakya might have been one of these authors.

Chanakya Niti is a collection of aphorisms, said to be selected by Chanakya from the various shastras. The topics discussed are ethics, morality, governance and several others.

Chanakya is regarded as a great thinker and diplomat in

India. Many Indian nationalists regard him as one of the earliest people who envisaged the united India spanning the entire subcontinent. India's former National Security Advisor Shiv Shankar Menon praised Chanakya's Arthashastra for its clear and precise rules which apply even today. Furthermore, he recommended reading of the book for broadening the vision on strategic issues.

The diplomatic enclave in New Delhi is named Chanakyapuri in honour of Chanakya. Institutes named after him include Training Ship Chanakya, Chanakya National Law University and Chanakya Institute of Public Leadership. Chanakya Circle in Mysore has been named after him.

Several modern adaptations of the legend of Chanakya narrate his story in a semi-fictional form, extending these legends. In Chandragupta (1911), a play by Dwijendralal Ray, the Nanda king exiles his half-brother Chandragupta, who joins the army of Alexander the Great. Later, with help from Chanakya and Katyayan (the former Prime Minister of Magadha), Chandragupta defeats Nanda, who is put to death by Chanakya.

The reading of Chanakya Neeti is as relevant today as it was at the time it was written. This book is an attempt to bring the same to the readers of today.

The Individual

(The basic purpose of Chanakya-Niti is to impart knowledge on every practical aspect of life. And in this context, he has touched upon various factors dealing with faith and culture, from the individual's point of view.)

Riches, vitality, life, body–all are fickle and fey; only Dharma is constant and everlasting.

*

God's abode is not the idols of wood, stone or earth. He dwells only in feeling.

*

But, even if one puts one's faith in the idols of gods made of metal, wood or stone and worshipsthem with total devotion, one is awarded with the desired result.

*

Anger is death, Lust is (the river of hell) Vaitarani, Knowledge is the cow of plenty and Satisfaction is (the divine orchard) Nandanvan.

Prayer

प्रणम्य शिरसा विष्णुं त्रैलोक्याधिपतिं प्रभुम्।
नाना शास्त्रोद्धृतं वक्ष्ये राजनीति समुच्चयम्।। 1 ।।

Pranammya Shirsaa Vishnum Trailokyaadhipatim Prabhum.
Naanaa Shaastroddhrootam Vikshye Rajneeti Samuchchyam.

I salute to the Lord of the three realms, Lord Vishnu, and now commence to describe the principles of the statecraft culled from various ancient books of knowledge.

धर्मेतत्परता मुखे मधुरता दाने समुत्साहता
मित्रोऽवञ्चकता गुरौ विनयता चितेऽपि गम्भरता।
आचरे शुचिता गुणे रिसकता शास्त्रोषु विज्ञातृता
रूपे सुन्दरता शिवे भनता त्वयस्ति भो राघव।। 2 ।।

Dharme Tattpartaa Mukhe Madhurtaa Daane Samuttsaahataa
Mittreavanchakataa Guru Vinyataa Chitteapi Gambheerataa.
Aachaare Shuchitaa Gune Rasiktaa Shaastreshu Vigyataa
Roope Sundartaa Shive Bhajantaa Tvayasti Bho Raaghav.

Devotion in faith, sweetness in voice, alacrity in alms-giving, guilelessness in relation with friends, humility for the Guru, depth in character; piety in behaviour, regard for merit, erudition in scriptural knowledge, beauty in appearance and belief in Lord Shiva (or in the welfare of all) are, O Raghav (Lord Rama), your attributes!

काष्ठं कल्पतरू: सुमेरूरचलश्चिन्तामणि: प्रस्तर:
सूर्यस्तीव्रकर: शशि: क्षयक निरवारिधि:।
कामो नष्टतनुर्बलिर्दितिसुतो नित्य पशु: कामगो:
नैतास्ते तुलयामि भो रघपते कस्योपभा दीयते।। 3 ।।

Kaashtham Kalpataruh Sumerurachalashinintaamanih Prashtarah
Soonyasteevrakarah Shashih Kshayakarah Kshaarohi Nirvaaridhih.
Kaamo Nashtatanurbalirditishuto Nittya Prashuh Kaamagoh
Naittaaste Tulayaami Bho Raghupate Kassyopabhaa Deeyate.

Kalpataru (The divine tree fulfilling all desires) is wooden: the Sumeru is a hill, the philosopher's stone is but a stone; the sun has scorching rays, the moon is waxing and waining, the sea (water) is saline, the Kamadeva (the god of love) is bodyless; Bali is a demon, the cow of plenty is an animal--

O Ram! I fail to compare you with anyone (i.e., everything with best of the attributes have some inherent defect in it): You are incomparable.

का चिन्ता मम जीवने यदि हरिर्विश्वम्भ्रो गीयते
नो चेदर्भकजीवनार्थ जनीस्तन्यं कुथं नि:सरेत्।
इत्यालोच्य मुहुर्महुर्यदु पते लक्ष्मीपते केवलं
त्वत्पादाम्बुजसेवनेन सततं कालो मया नीयते।। 4 ।।

Kaa chintaa Mam Jeevane Yadi Harirvishvambharo geeyate
No chedarbhakjeevanaarth Jananeestannyam Kutham Nihsaret.
Ittyaalochaya Muhurmuhuryadu Pate Laxmipate Kevalam
Tvattapaadaambujsevanen Satatam Kaalo Mayaa Neeyate.

Why should I worry for life as Lord Hari is the sustainer of the world. Had it not been so then how come a mother's breasts be filled with milk for her infant automatically? Believing this (that he who creates life also provides for its sustenance) O spouse of Lakshmi! I pass my life devoted to your feet!

God

पुष्पे गन्ध्र तिले तैलं काष्ठे वह्निः पयोघृतम्।
इक्षो गुड़ं तथादेहे पश्यात्मानं विवेकत:।। 5 ।।

Pushpe Gandham Tile Tailam Kaashthe Vahannih Payoghritam.
Ikshau Gudam Tathaa Dehe Pashyaattmanam Vivekatah.

God dwells in our bodies, life fragrance in flowers, oil in oil seeds, fire in wood, ghee in milk, jaggery in the sugarcane. The wise should understand this.

न देवो विद्यते काष्ठे न पाषाणे न मृण्मये।
भावे ही विद्यते देवस्तस्माद भावो ही कारणाम् ।। 6।।

Na Devo Viddyate Kaashthe Na Paashaane Na Mrinnyamaye.
Bhave Hee Viddyate Devastsmaad Bhaavo Hee Kaaranam.

God doesn't dwell in the wooden, stony or earthen idols. His abode is in our feelings, our thoughts. [It is only through the feeling that we deem God existing in these idols.]

अग्निहोत्रं बिना वेदा: न च दानं बिना क्रिया।
न भावेन बिना सिद्धिस्तस्माद्द भावो ही कारणम् ।। 7 ।।

Agnihottram Binaa Vedaah Na cha Daanam Bina Kriyaa.
Na Bhaaven Bina Siddhistasmaad Bhaavo Hee Kaaranam.

Studying the Vedas without maintaining the sacred fire and offering oblation to it is as useless as performing the sacrifice without giving alms. One must attempt with feeling of total devotion to get success in any venture.

काष्ठपाषाणं धतूनां कृत्वा भावेन सेवनम्।
श्रद्धया च तथा सिद्धिस्तस्य विश्णो: प्रसादत: ।। 8 ।।

Kaashthapaashaanam Dhaatunaam Krittvaa Bhaaven Sevanam.
Shraddhayaa Cha Tathaa Siddhistasya Vishnoh Prasasadatah.

If one worships even the wooden, stony or the metallic idols with feeling, then by the grace of God one gets the desired objects or adeptness.

अग्निर्देवों द्विजातीनां मनीषिणं दि दैवतम्।
प्रतिमा स्वल्पबुद्धीनां सर्वत्रा समदर्शिन: ।। 9 ।।

Agnirdevo Dvijaatinaam Maneeshinaam Hridim Daivatam.
Pratimaa Svalpabhuddheenaam Sarvatra Samadarshinah.

The deity of the Twice-born(brahmans) is fire. The wise behold their deity inside their hearts. Those with lesser intelligence deem deity existing in the idols and those viewing the world impartially behold their deity permeating the whole world.

कलौ दशसहस्त्राणि हरिस्तयजति मेदिनीम्।
तदद्दर्धे जावी तोयं तदद्दर्धे ग्र्रामदेवता।। 10 ।।

Kalan Dashasahastraani Haristasyajati Modineem.
Tadaddardhe Jaahavee Toyam Tadaadaardhe Graamdevataa

Lord Hari (vishnu) leaves the earth after completing ten thousand years of the Kaliyuga: the Ganga withdraws her waters after comple ting half of this period [i.e., five thousand years of the Kaliyuga[and the Gramdevtas (local deities) leave the earth after completing half of this period

(i.e., two thousand five hundred years of the Kaliyuga.)

DHARM

चला लक्ष्मीश्चला: प्राणाश्चले जीवितमन्दिरे।
चलाचले च संसारे धर्म एको हि निश्चल: ।। 11 ।।

Chalaa Laxmishchalaah Praanaashchale Jeevitmandire.
Chalaachale cha Sansaare Dharma Eko Hi Nishchalah.

All riches, vitality, life and body are fickle and fey: Only the Dharma is constant and everlasting.

अनित्यानि शरीराणि विभवो नैव शाश्वत:।
नित्यं सन्निहितो मृत्यु: कर्तव्यो धर्मसंग्रह: ।। 12 ।।

Anittyaani Shareeraani Vibhvo Naiv Saashvatah.
Nittyam Sannihito Mrittuh Kartavyo Dharmasangrah.

Constantly bounded by death, all power and pelf are fey. Hence one should adhere to one's Dharma, which is everlasting.

जीवन्तं मृतवन्मन्ये देहनं धर्मवर्जितम्।
मृतो धर्मेणसंयुक्तो दीर्घजीवी न संशय: ।। 13 ।।

Jeevantam Mritvannamannye Dehinam Dharmavarjitam Mrito
Dharmen Sanyuto Deerghajeevee Na Sanshayah.

I deem as dead a being devoid of Dharma! He who adheres to one's Dharma is long-aged even if he is dead – there is no doubt about it!

Consequence of an Action

यथा धेनु सहस्त्रेषु वत्सो गच्छति मातरम्।
तथा यच्च कृतं कर्म कर्तारम नुगच्छति।। 14 ।।

Yathaa Dhenu Sahastreshu Vattso Gachhati Maatram.
Tathaa Yachcha Kritam Karma Kartaaramanugachchati.

Like a calf finds the mother-cow even it there be thousands of cows, so the consequence of an action searches its doer unerringly.

[i.e., one can't escape the consequence of an action do whatever one may.]

स्वयं कर्म करोत्यात्मा स्वंय तत्पफलमश्नुते।
स्वयं भ्रमति संसारे स्वंय तस्माद्विमुच्चते।। 15 ।।

Svayam Karma Karottyaattamaa Svayam Tattphalamashnute
Svayam Bhramati Sansaare Svayam Tasmaaddvimuchchayate.

Man himself does action and himself bears its consequences. He himself roams about in the world and gets liberated from this cycle of birth and death

[Chanakya says that man is free to act but he must bear its consequences, whether good or bad. It is only his balance-sheet of the action and its consequence has been set at naught that he becomes liberated. Hence to achieve this liberation is also well within the control of man.]

कर्मायतं फलं पुसां बुद्धिः कमा्रनुसारिणी।
तथापि सुध्यिाचार्यः सुविचार्येव कुर्वते।। 16 ।।

Karmaayattam Phalam Pusaani Buddhih Karmaanusaarini.
Tathapi Sudhiyaachaaryaah Suvichaaryava Kurvate.

Although man reaps as he sows and his wisdom is also controlled by his action, yet the prudent and wisemen act very thoughtfully, fully weighing the good and bad consequences. [It means that though the resultant of the deeds committed in previous life decide the good and bad consequence in this life, still one must act after a thoughtful deliberation.

आत्मापराध्वृक्षस्य पफलान्येतानि देहिनाम्।
दारिद्रयरोग दुःखानि बन्ध्नव्यसनानानि च ।। 17 ।।

Aattmaaparaadhavrikshasya Phalaanyetaani Dehinaam.
Daaridrayarogah Duhkhaani Bandhanvuasnaani cha.

Poverty, disease, grief, bondage and all the infatuative addictions are the fruits of the tree of sin of a person.

जन्मजन्मनि चाभ्यस्तंदानमययन तपः।
तेनैवाभ्यासयोन देही वाभ्यस्यते ।। 18 ।।

Janmajanmani Chaabhyastam Daanmaddhyayan Taphah.
Tenaivaabhyaasyagen Dehi Vaabhyaste.

It is after the constant practice of many lives that man attains to the capacity to learn, to do penance or to dole out alms.

Luck or Fate

आयु: कर्म वितच विद्या निध्रमेव च
पचतानि हि सृज्यन्ते गर्भस्थस्यैव देहिन: ।। 19 ।।

Aayuh Karma Vittancha Viddyaa Nidhanmeva cha.
Panchtaani Hi Srijjyante Garbhasthasyaiv Dehinah.

Age, profession, financial status, level of education and death – these five basic parameters of human life are ordained when the being is in the embryonic form.

रंक करोति राजानं राजानं रंकमेव च।
धनिनं निर्धनचैव निर्धन धनिनं विधि:।। 20 ।।

Ranka Karoti Raajaanam Rajaanam Rankmev Cha.
Dhaninam Nirdhanam Chaiv Nirdhanam Dhaninam vidhih

.

It is one's fate that makes a beggar a king or a king a beggar; a rich man a pauper or a pauper rich.

पत्रां नैव यवा करीरविट पे दोषो वसन्तस्य किं
नोलूकोप्यवलोकयते यदि दिवा सूर्यस्य किं द्रूषणाम?
वर्षा नैव पतति चातकमुखे मेघस्य कि द्रूषणाम्
यत्पूर्व विधिना ललाट लिखितं तन्मार्जितु क:क्षम:? ।। 21 ।।

Patram Naiv Yava Karreravit Pe dosho Vasantasya kim
Nollokaappyavalokayate Yadi Diva Sooryasya Kim Dooshanam?
Varshaa naiv Patati Chaatakmukhe Meghasya Kim Dooshanam.
Yattpoorva Vidhinaa Lalaat Likhitam Tanmanaarjitu Kah Kshamah?

If leaves do not sprout in the Kareel (Capparis ahpylla) tree, is it the flaw of the Spring Season? If an owl fails to see in daylight, is it the flaw of the sun ? If the rain- drop doesn't fall in the mouth of Chatak

(Cuculus melanoleucus) is it the flaw of the clouds? Who can alter the fate ordained as the destiny? [Chanakya says that individual deficiency is caused by destiny for which external a circumstances cannot be held responsible.]

ईपि्सतं मनस: सर्व कस्य सम्पद्यते सुखम्।
दैवायतं यत: सर्व तस्मात् सन्तोषमाश्रयेत् ।। 22 ।।

Eepsitam Mansah Sarva Kasya Sampaddyate Sukham.
Daivaayattam Yatah Sarva Tasmaat Santoshmaashrayet.

Who gets all that one aspires for? Everything one gets is what is destined for one. Hence all must seek satisfaction in whatever they receive.

Self-welfare

यावत्स्वस्थो ह्यायं देह: तावन्मृत्युश्च दूरत:।
तावदात्महितं कुर्यात् प्राणान्तें किं करिष्यति।। 23 ।।

Yaavattsvastho Yahayam Dehah Taavanmriuttushcha Dooratah.
Taavdaattmahitam Kuryaat Praanante Kim Karishyati.

Death is away till one's body is healthy. Hence one should achieve one's welfare till one is healthy, for death ceases all activities.

Self-knowledge

नास्ति काम समो व्याधिर्नास्ति मोहसमो रिपुः।
नास्ति कोप समो वह्निः नास्ति ज्ञानात्परं सुखम्।। 24 ।।

Naasti Kaam Samo Vyaadhirnaasti Mohasamo Ripuh.
Naasti Kop Samo Vahinnih Naasti Gyaanaattparam Sulkham.

No disease is more deadly than (the sexual) desire, no enemy is more dangerous than infatuation, no fire is hotter than the fire of wrath and no happiness is better than the self-knowledge.

Truth

सत्येन धर्यति पृथ्वी सत्येन तपते रविः।
सत्येन वाति वायुश्च सर्वसत्ये प्रतिष्ठितम्।। 25 ।।

Sattyen Dhaaryate Prithvee Sttyen Tapate Ravi
Sattyen Vaati Vaayushcha Sarvam Sattye Prathishthitam.

Truth stabilises the world, makes the sun shine and the wind blow. Truth establishes well everything in life.

[Chanakya says that truth alone establishes the order in the Creation.]

Destiny

तादृशी जायते बुद्धिर्व्यवसायोऽपि तादृशः।
सहायास्तादृशा: एव यादृशी भवितव्यता ।।। 26 ।।

Taadrishee Jaayte Buddhivaryavsaayoapi Taadrishah.

Sahaayaasstaadrishaah Eva Yaadrishee Bhavitavyataa.

One gets everything according to 'one's destiny. One's action, response, reaction–all are guided by the factors of destiny.

[meaning the rule of destiny is supreme in human life. If one is destined to reap a good harvest one would get situation conductive to his receiving good result and vice versa.]

Moksha (Liberation)

मुक्तिमिच्छसि चेत्तत विषयान् विषवत् त्यज।
क्षमार्जवदयाशैचं सत्यं पीयूषवत् पिब ।। 27 ।।

Muktimichasi Cheetat Vishayaan Vishvat Tyaji.
Kshamaarjvadyaashaucham Sattyam Peeyooshvat Pib.

O dear, if you really seek liberation of your soul then shun all the sensual attractions as though they are poison and cultivate the spirit of forgiveness, the rectitude of conduct, compassion, piety truth and similar other qualities which are nectar for human life.

बन्धाय विषयासंग: मुकत्यै निर्विषयं मन:।
मनएवं मनुष्याणां कारणं बन्धमोक्षयों: ।। 28 ।।

Bandhanaaya Vishyaasangah Muktayai Nirvishyam Manah.
Man Eva Manusshyaanaam Kaaranam Bandmokshyoh.

Bondage is indulgence in vices and renunciation of them is liberation. Thus it is mind, which drives one to bondage or to liberation.

Samadhi (Meditation)

> देहाभिमानगलिते ज्ञानेन परमात्मनः।
> यत्रा-यत्रा मनो याति तत्रा-तत्रा समाध्यः।। 29 ।।

Dehaabhimaangalite Gyaanen Paramaattmanah.
Yatra-Yatro Mano Yaati Tatra-Tatra Samaadhayah.

The communion with, and realisation of God, melts away the arrogance of the physical attributes. Achieving this stage, one is able to concentrate easily in meditation, wherever and whenever one wants.

Vairagya (Aversion to the Temporal World)

> धर्माख्याने श्मशाने च रोगिणां या मतिर्भवेत्।
> सा सर्वदैव तिष्ठेच्चेत् को न मुच्येत बन्धात्।। 30 ।।

Dharmakkhyaane Shmashaane Cha Roginaam Yaa Matirbhavet.
Saa Sarvadaiv Thishttbechchet Ko Na Muchyate Bandhanaat

One develops a version to the temporal world by listening to the sacred tales, viewing the diseased persons and visiting the crematorium. And if one remains averse to wordly considerations, he is bound to be free from all the bondages.

Soul

पुष्पे गन्धं तिले तैल काष्ठे वह्निः पयोघृतम्।
इक्षौ गुड़ं तथा देहे पश्यात्मानं विवेकतः ।। 31 ।।

Pushpe Gandham Tile Tail Kaashthe VAhinah Payoghritam.
Ekshau Gudam Tathaa Dehe Pasyaatmaanam Vivektah.

Discern soul in the body like you feel fragrance in flower, oil in the oilseed. fire in wood, ghee in milk and jaggery in sugarcanes.

Quietude

यस्तु संवत्सरं पूर्ण नित्यं मौनेन भुञ्जते।
युगकोटिसहस्त्रान्तु स्वर्गलोके महीयते ।। 32 ।।

Yastu Samvattsaram Poorna Nittyam Maunen Bhunjate.
Yugkotisahastrantu Svargaloke Meheeyate.

He, who eats his meals qui etly throughout the year, earns the merit, deserve his stay for thousands of epochs in the heaven.

यद् द्वूरं यद् दुराराधं यच्च द्वूरे व्यवस्थितम्।
तत्सर्व तपसा साध्यं तपो हि दुरतिक्रमम्।। 33 ।।

Yaddooram Yadduraaraaddhyam Yachcha Doore Vyavasthitam.
Tattsarva Tapasaa Saaddhyam Tapo hi Duratikramam.

Even if the destination or the desired object be far away or difficult to achieve one can reach it or get it if one is determined. Nothing is impossible for a determined person.

Restraint

इन्द्रियाणि च संयम्य बक वत् पण्डितो नरः।
देशकाल बलं ज्ञात्वा सर्वकार्याणि साध्येत् ।। 34 ।।

Indrayaani Cha Samyamya Bak vat Pandito Narah.
Deshkaal balam Gyattva Sarvakaaryaani Saadhyet.

The wise man should put restraint on his sensual desires to control them and then only he should accomplish his work after assessing his strength in the context of time and space

[i.e., after cutting off the distraction caused by the sensual deviations, the wise man should enhance his strength to the hilt and then he should assess his position vis-a-vis the place and time he has to accompish his work in.]

The Only Way

यदीच्छसि वशीकर्तु जगदेकेनकर्मणा।
परापवादशास्त्रोभ्यो गां चरन्तीं निवरय।। 35 ।।

Yaddeechachasi Vasheekartu Jagadeken Karmana.
Paraapavaadashaastreebhyo Gaam Charanteem Nivaarya.

If you want to overpower the entire world merely by just one action, then put restraint upon your tongue speaking ill of others.

WHO'S WHO

क्रोधो वैवस्वतो राजा तृष्णा वैतरणी नदी।
विद्या कामदुघा धेनुः संतोषो नन्दनं वनम् ।। 36 ।।

Krodho Vaivasvato Raajaa Trishnaa Vaitarnee Nadee.
Viddyaa Kaamdudhaadhenuh Santosho Nandanam Vanam.

Anger is death (i.e., lord of death Yamraj Vaivaswat), lust is (the river of hell) Vaitarani, knowledge is the cow of plenty and satisfaction is (the divine orchard) Nandanvan.

शान्तितुल्यं तपो नास्ति त सनतोषात्परं सुखम्।
न तृष्णया परो व्याधिर्न च धर्मो दयापरः ।। 37 ।।

Shaantitullyam Tapo Naasti Na Santoshaatparamsukham.
Na Trishnayaaparo Vyaadhirnacha Dharmo Dayaaparah.

No penance is greater than the one done for maintaining peace, no happiness is better than the one received from satisfaction, no disease is more damaging than greed and no Dharma is better than the one having compassion for all.

यस्य चितं द्रवीभूतं कृपया सर्वजन्तुषु।
तस्य ज्ञानेने मोक्षेण कि जटा भस्मलेपनैः ।। 38 ।।

Yasya Chittam Draveebhootam Kripayaa Sarvajantushu.
Tasya Gyanen Mokshena Kim Jataa Bhasmalepanaih.

He, whose heart is full of compassion for all beings, does not need to seek any other knowledge, or Moksha (liberation) or care for rubbing ash all over his body (like the celebrated hermits).

ALMS-GIVING AND DONATION

देयं भोज्यधनं सुकृतिभिर्नो संचयस्तस्य वै,
श्रीकर्णस्य बलेश्च विक्रमपतेरद्यापि कीर्ति स्थिता।
अस्मकं मधुदानयोगरहितं नष्ट चिरात्संचित:
निर्वाणादिति नष्टपादयुगलं घर्षत्यमी मक्षिका: ।। 39 ।।

Deyam Bhojyadhanam Sukritibhirno Sanchayastasya Vai.
Shri Karnassya Baleshcha Vikrampatreddyapi Keerti Sthitaa.
Asmaakam Madhudaanyogarahitam Nashtam Chiraatsanchitaah
Nirvaanaaditi Nashtapaadyugalam Gharshttyamee Makshikaah.

All great men should donate eatables and wealth. It is improper to hoard these things. The fame of Karna (of Mahabharat) and Bali (a mythological monarch renowned for his sacrifice and charity) is still unblemished because of their acts of charity. The honeybees ruefully rub their feet against ground. They neither enjoy their honey nor gifting it to others.

[Chanakya uses an allegory to bring home his point. He says the honeybees do not eat the honey, they neither collect nor give it to others. And when a person takes away their honey they fall to the ground in utter frustration.]

आर्तेषु विप्रेशु दयान्विश्चेच्छद्धेन य: स्वल्पमुपैति दानम्।
अनन्तपारं समुपैति दानं यद्दीयते तन्न लभेद्द द्विजेभ्य: ।। 40 ।।

Aarteshu Vipreshu Dayaannivihschechaddhena Yaha Svalpamupaiti Daanam.
Anantparam Samupaiti Daanam Yaddeeyate Tanna Labhed Dvijebhyah.

He who gives gifts and donations to the distressed and the learned gets back his these gifts many times over

[i.e., they earn great merit by these gifts because by helping- them they not only preserve life knowledge but also help in their growth.]

Gift to the Deserving

> क्षीयन्ते सर्वदानानि यज्ञ होमबलि क्रियाः।
> न क्षीयते पात्रादानमभयं सर्वदिहिनाम् ।। 41 ।।

Ksheeyante Sarvadaanaani Yagya Homabali Kriyaah.
Na Ksheeyate Paatradaanambhayam Sarvadehinaam.

All sacrifices, gifts, donations, etc., vanish in their effect after sometime but that which is given to a deserving person survive for ever. Because the deserving receiver utilises the gifts best to further this chain of charity for the welfare of all.

Donate Liberally!

> सन्तोषस्त्रिषु कर्तव्यः स्वदारे भोजने घने।
> त्रिषुचैव नकर्तव्योऽध्ययने जपदानयोः ।। 42 ।।

Santoshstrishu Kartavyah Svadaare Bhojane Ghane.
Trishuchaiv Na Kartavyoaddhyayane Japadaanayoh.

One should always be satisfied (i) with his wife, (ii) with his diet and (iii) with his wealth; but never with (i) his studies, (ii) his austerity and penance and (iii) with his donations and gifts to the deserving persons.

Mother, the Supreme God

नान्नोदकसमं दानं न तिथिद्‌र्वादशी समा।
न गायात्रया: पर मत्रो नमातुदैर्वतें परम्‌ ॥ 43॥

Naannodakasamam Daanam Na Tithiddrvaadashee Samaa.
Na Gaayattryaah Paro Mantro Na Maturdaivatam Param.

No gift is better than the gift of cereal and water, no date is better than the Dwadashi (the twelfth day of the lunar calendar); no Mantra is greater than the Gayatri-Mantra and no god is greater than mother.

राजपत्नी गुरो: पत्नी मित्रापत्नी तथैव च।
पत्नीमाता स्वमाता च पञ्चैता: मातर: स्मृता: ॥ 44 ॥

Raajpatnee Guroh Patnee Mitrapatnee Tathaiv Cha.
Patneemaataa Svamaataa Cha Panchaittah Maatarah Smritah.

The wife of the king, the wife of the guru, the wife of the friend, the mother of wife and one's own mother – these five ladies deserve the status of mother.

FATHER, THE GUIDE

जनिता चोपनेता च यस्तु विद्यां प्रयच्छति।
अन्नदाता भयत्राता पचैता पितरः स्मृताः ।। 45 ।।

Janitaa Chopanetaa Cha Yastu Viddyam Prayachhati.
Annadaataa Bhayatraataa Panchaitaa Pitrah Smritaah.

The one who gives birth to you, the one who gets your Upanayan (Sacred Thread) ceremony performed, the one who gives you education, the one who gives you food and the one who protects you from all sort of dangers – these five persons deserve the status of your father !

पुनश्च विविधैः शीलैर्नियोज्य सतत बुधै।
नीतिज्ञा शीलसम्पन्नाः भविष्यन्ति कुलपूजिताः ।। 46 ।।

Punashcha Vividhaih Sheelairniyojjyaa Satatam Budhai.
Neetiggyaa Seelasampannaah Bhavishyanti Kulpoojitaah.

A wise father must educate his son, in a variety of ways, in making him learn good manners, develop good character and get good knowledge, etc.; because the noble son brings glory to the family and win admiration of their brethren.

लालयेत् पंचवषाणि दशवर्षीणि ताडयेत्।
प्राप्त तु षोडशे वर्षे पुत्रां मित्रावदाचरेत् ।। 47 ।।

Laalyet Panchavarshani Dashavarshaani Taadyet.
Praapte tu Shodashe Varshe Putram Mitravadaacharet.

Rear up your son affectionately till he is five year old then admonish him strictly for next ten years. When he turns sixteen, start treating him as your friend.

The Worthy Son

एकेनापि सुपत्रोण विद्यायुक्ते च साधुना।
आल्हादितं कुलं सर्व यचिन्द्रेण शर्वरी ।। 48।।

Ekenaapi Suputrena Viddyayukte Cha Sadhuna.
Aahladitam Kulam Sarva Yatha Chandren Sharvari.

A wise, well educated and worthy son alone is enough to bring glory to the family like the lonely moon is enough to bedight the night with charms.

एकेनापि सुपत्रोण पुष्पितेनसुगंधिना।
वसितं तद्वनं सर्व सुपुत्रोण कुलं यथा ।। 49।।

Ekenaapi Suputren Pushpiten Sugandhinaa.
Vasitam Taddvanam Sarva Suputren Kulam Yatha.

One well blossomed and sweet smelling flower is enough to turn the whole garden fragrant. Similarly, one worthy son is enough to bring glory to the whole family.

कि जातैर्बहुभि: पुत्रौ: शोकसन्तापकारकै:।
वरमेक: कुलावलम्बी यत्र विश्राम्यते कुलम्।। 50।।

Kim Jaatairbahurbhih Putraih Shoksantaapkaarkaih.
Varmekah Kulaavalambi Yatra Vishraammyate Kulam.

No use having many sons causing worry and sorrow. One worthy son is enough who may support the entire family.

एकोऽ गुणवान पुत्राः निर्गुणैश्च शतैर्वरम्।
एकश्चन्द्रस्तमो हन्दि न च तारा सहस्त्राशः ।। 51।।

Ekoapi Gunavaan Putrah Nirgunaisheha Shatairvaram.
Ekashchandramasto Hantinacha Taaraa Shastrashah.

One worthy son is better than a hundred incompetent and useless sons. The moon is capable enough of destroying the darkness, which even thousands of stars fail to achieve.

The Incompetent Son

एकेन शुष्कवृक्षेण दह्यमानेन।
दह्यते तद्वनं सर्व कुपुत्रोण कुलं यथा।। 52।।

Eken Shuskvrikshen Dahiyamaanen Vahinnanaa.
Dahyate Taddvanam Sarva Kuputren Kulam Yathaa.

Just as, one dry tree on catching fire can burn the whole orchard to ashes, similarly, one incompetent and bad son ruins the entire family.

कि तया क्रियते धेन्वा या न दोग्ध्री न गर्भिणी।
कोऽर्थः पुत्रोण जातेन यो न विद्वान्न भक्तिामन् ।। 53।।

Ki tayaa Kriyate Dhennvaa Yaana Doggdhree na Garbhinee.
Koarthah Putren Jaaten Yon a Viddvaana Bhaktimaan.

What value is of that cow, which neither conceives nor gives milk? The same way what worth is of that son who is neither educated (or a scholar) nor devoted to God?

मूर्खश्चिरायुर्जातोऽपि तस्माज्जातान्मृतो वरम्।
मृतःस चाल्पदुःखाय यावज्जीवं जडो दहेत् ।। 54 ।।

Moorkhashchiraayurjaatoapi Tassmaattjaataannmrito Varam.
Mritahsa Chalpadukhaaya Vavajjeevam Jado Dahet.

It is better for a foolish son to die early rather than survive long, because by dying he would give sorrow only once but by surviving he would cause grief and sorrow every moment of his survival by his repeated acts of foolishness. A worthless son is better dead than alive.

Wife

सा भार्या या शुचिदक्षस भार्या या पतिव्रता।
सा भार्या या पतिप्रीता सा भार्या सत्यवादिनीः ।। 55 ।।

Saa Bhaaryaa Shuchidakshaa Saa Bhaaryaa Yaa Pativratta.
Saa Bhaaryaa Yaa Patipreetaa saa Bhaaryaa Sttyavaadineehee.

(True) wife is that who is pious and deft (in her work), who is faithful to her husband, who loves her husband and who is truthful to her husband. [Chanakya lists five qualities for an ideal wife: she ought to be pious, deft, faithful, loving and truthful to her husband.]

पत्युराज्ञां बिना नारी उपोष्य व्रतचारिणी।
आयुष्य हरते भर्तु:सा नारी नरकं व्रजेत् ।।56।।

Patturaagyaam Binaa Naaree Uposhya Vratchaarinee.
Aayushya Harte Bhartuhsaa Naaree Narakam Vrajet.

That wife who takes a resolve without seeking her husband's permission for it verily shortens her husband's life. Such women are consigned to hell when they die.

Woman

स्त्रीणा द्विगुण अहारो लज्जा चापि चतुर्गुणा।
साहसं षडगुणं चैव कामश्चाष्टगुण: स्मृत: ।।57।।

Streenaa Dvigun Ahaaro Lajjaa Chaapi Chaturgunaa.
Saahasam Shadgunam Chaiv Kaamashchachaashatgunah Smritah.

(In comparison to a man) A woman is having two times more appetite, four times more shyness, six times more courage and eight times more the sexual desire.

अनृतं साहसं माय मूर्खत्वमतिलोभिता।
अशौचत्वं निर्दयत्वं स्त्रीणां दोषा: स्वभावजा: ।।58।।

Anritam Saahasam Maayaa Moorkhattvamatilobhitaa.
Asshauchaatvam Nirdayattvam Streenaam Doshaah Svabhaavajaah.

A woman, by nature, is liar, courageous, deceitful, foolish, greedy, impious and cruel. These are the innate attributes of a woman.

वित्तेन रक्ष्यते धर्मो विद्या योगेन रक्ष्यते।
मृदुना रक्ष्यते भूपः सतिस्त्रया रक्ष्यते गृहम् ।। 59।।

Vittyen Rakshayate Dharmo Viddya Yogen Rakshayate.
Mridunaa Rakshayate Bhoopah Satishtriyah Rakshatate Griham.

Wealth protects Dharma, Yoga protects education or knowledge, suavity protects king and a good woman protects home. [Chanakya says that for maintaining Dharma some material resources are needed which can be procured only by money; Yoga here means application. Obviously, knowledge decays when not applied. According to Chanakya a rough – tough ruler is ill suited for the job. It is only by suavity or apparent softness that he can win over people easily. The last observation is too true to need any clarification.

न दानात् शुद्धत्रते नारी नोपवोसैः शतैरपि।
न तीर्थसेवया तद्वद् भर्तुः पादोदकैर्यथा ।। 60।।

Na Daanaat Shuddhatrate Naaree Vopvasaih Shatairaop.
Na Teerthasevayaa Taddvad Bhartuh Paadodakairyathaa.

A women doesn't become as pious by giving alms, performing rigid austerities and fasts and visiting sacred places as by having the water she gets after washing her husband's feet.

यो मोहयन्मन्यते मूढ़ो रक्तेयं मयि कामिनी।
स तस्य वशगो भृत्वा नृत्येत् क्रीडा शकुन्तवत् ।। 61।।

Yo Mohayanmannyate Moodho Rakteyam Mayi Kaamine.
Sa Tassya Vashago Bhrittva Nrityet Kreedaa Shakurtavat.

The foolish man who, under the infatuation, believes that a particular beautiful woman has fallen for him verily dances to her tune as though he is her plaything!

जल्पन्ति सार्धमन्येन पश्यन्त्यन्यं सविभ्रमाः।
हृदये चिन्तयन्त्यन्यं न स्त्रीणामेकतो रतिः ।।62।।

Jalpanti Saardhamannyen Pashyanttyannyam Savibhramaah.
Hridaye Chintayanttyaannyam Na Streenaamekato Ratih.

Women have a knack of talking to one man, casting an askew glance at other and loving secretly a third man. They can't devotedly love just one man.

वरयेत्कुलजां प्राज्ञो निरूपामापि कन्यकाम्।
रूपशीलां न नीचस्यां विवाहः सदृशे कुले ।।63।।

Varyettkuljaam Praggyo Niroopaamapi Kannyakkam.
Roopsheelaam Na Neechassyaam Vivaah Sadrishe Kule.

A wiseman shouldn't hesitate marrying an ugly girl, if she happens to belong to a reputed good family. But if a girl is extremely beautiful, the wiseman shouldn't marry her if she is from a lowly, illreputed family. A matromonial alliance is best established between the families of equal status.

विषादप्यमृतं ग्राह्यममेध्यादपि कांचनम्।
नीचादप्युत्तमां विद्यां स्त्रीरत्नं दुष्कुलादपि ।।64।।

Vishaadppyamritam Graahyamameddhyaadapi Kaanchanam.
Neechadappyuttamaam Viddyaam Streeratnam Dushkulaadapi.

Do not hesitate in getting nectar even from poision if it be available and gold even from the filth. Accept good knowledge even from a pariah and good girl even from a low family.

[Both these aphorisms state contradictory observations. While the above one says don't marry a girl from a low family even if she be good and virtuous, the Shloka below asserts marrying a virtuous girl even if belonging to low caste or a low family].

The Parents

माता शत्रुः पिता वैरी येन बालो न पाठितः।
न शोभते सभामये हंसमये बको यथा ।। 65 ।।

Maataa Shatruh Pitaa Vairee Yen Baalo Na Pathitaha.
Na Shobhate Sabhaa Maddhye Hansamddhye Bako Yathaa.

Those parents who don't take interest in their son's education (or who don't provide him with good education) are verily his enemies. An illiterate man among the literate ones looks as ugly as a crow among the swans.

ऋण्कर्ता पिता शत्रुर्माता च व्यभिचारिणी।
भार्या रूपवती शत्रुः पुत्र शत्रु न पंडितः ।। 66 ।।

Rinakartaa Pitaa Shatrurmaataa Cha Vyabhichaarinee.
Bhaaryaa Roopavatee Shatruh Putrashatnurn Panditah.

A father bequeathing the loan; a mother of loose morals;

a wife extremely beautiful and a foolish son – all should be deemed as enemies.

Mutual Relationship

ते पूत्रा ये पितृभक्ता स पिता यस्तु पोषकः ।
तन्मित्राम् यत्रा विश्वासः सा भार्या या निवृत्तिः ।। 67 ।।

Te Putra Ye Pitrabhakta Sa Pita Yastu Poshakah.
Tanmitram Yatra Vishvaasah Saa Bharyaa Yaa Nivratih.

The (real) son is he who is devoted to his father; the (real) father is he who looks after his son well and rears him up with care; the (real) friend is who is trusted one and the (real) wife is she who delights her husband's heart.

Home

यदि रामा यदि च रमा यदि तनयो विनयगणोपेतः ।
तनयो तनयोत्पत्तिः सुरवरनगरे किाध्क्यिम् ।। 68 ।।

Yadi Raamaa Yadi Cha Ramaa Yad Tanya Vinay Ganopetah.
Tanyo Tanyotpattih Survarnagare Kimaadhikkyam.

That home, beats even the divine pleasures hollow which has a virtuous lady, a noble-natured and promising son with his own son (grandson) and enough riches.

न विप्रपादोदक पंकिलानि
न वेदशास्त्रावनिगर्जितानि।
स्वाहास्वधकारवनिवर्जितानि
श्मशानतुल्यानि गृहाणि तानि ।। 69 ।।

Na Vipprapaadodak Pankilaani
Na Vedshaastraddhivanigarjtaani.
Svaahaasvadhaakaarddhvanivrajitaani
Shmashaantullyani Grihaani Taani.

That home which is not smeared by the mud and dust brought in by the scholarly brahman's feet; where no sound of chanting of the 'Veda-Mantras' is heard; from where the reverberations made at the time of offering oblation to the sacred fire: [SWAHA-SWAHA, etc.] do not originate is verily as inauspicious and eerie as a crematorium.

The Brahmans

विप्रो वृक्षस्तस्य मूलं सन्या
वेदाः शाखा धर्मकर्माणि पत्राम्।
तस्मान्मूलं यत्नतो रक्षणीयं
छिन्ने मूलं नैव शाखा न पत्राम् ।। 70 ।।

Vippro Vrikshasstaassya Moolam Sanddhya
Veddah Shaakhaa Dharmakarmaani Patram.
Tasmaannmoolam Yattnato Rakshaneeyam
Chhinne Moolen Naiv Shakhaa Na Patram.

The Vipra (scholarly brahmans) is the tree whose root is the Vedic Hymn chanted every evening and morning, worship the religious and ritual acts being the leaves. The root of the tree must be protected at every cost as the whole tree derive strength from it. If the root is lost then neither the leaves would remain nor the branches.

धन्या द्विजमयीं नौका विपरीता भवार्णवे।
तरन्तधेगता सर्वे उपस्थिता पतन्त्येव हि ।। 71 ।।

Dhannya Dvijamayeem Nauka Vipreetaa Bhavaarnave.
Tarannttyadhogataa Sarve Upasthitaa Patannyeva Hi.

This boat, in the form of the brahman, going across the sea of existence is typical as it moves in a reverse order. Those who remain below it go across easily but those who try to ride over it fall down and gets drowned

[It is a symbolic representation of the assertion that those who remain below the brahman's fair better in this mundane sea of existence and successfully cross at. But those who try to defy the authority of the brahmans meet their ruin.]

एकाहारेण सन्तुष्ट : षड्कर्मनिरतः सदा।
त्रातुकालेऽभिगामी च स विप्रो द्विज उच्चयते ।। 72 ।।

Ekahaaren Santushtah Shadkarmaniratah Sadda.
Ritukaaliabhigaamee Cha Sa Vippro Dvij Uchchyate.

That brahman who eats only once in the day, devotes his time in studies and in practising various austerities and who copulates with his wife only during her Ritu Kal (the period immediately after the menses is called the Dwij or the twice born).

अकृष्ट फलमूलानि वनवासरतः सदा।
कुरुतेऽहरहः श्राद्धमृषिर्विप्रः स उच्यते ।। 73 ।।

Akrishta Phalmoolani Vanvaasaratah Sadda.
Kurteaharh Shraaddhamishirvipprah Sa Uchchyate.

The brahman who eats only roots and bulbs produced from the land untilled, who ever dwells in jungles and performs the Shraaddha [of his departed ancestors] everyday is called a Rishi (sage).

लौकिके कर्मणि रतः पशूनां परिपालकः।
वाणिज्यकृषिकर्मा यः स विप्रो वैश्य उच्यते ।। 74 ।।

Laukike Karmaani Ratah Pashoonaam Paripaalakah.
Vaanijjyakrishikarmaa Yah Sa Vippro Vaishya Uchchyate.

The brahman who ever remains busy in the mundane work, who owns and tends to cattle; who tills the land and does farming is known as Vaishya (Merchant class) Brahman.

[Chanakya is trying to assert that one's social category is not defined by birth but by one's profession.]

लाक्षादि तैलनीलानां कौसुम्भमघुसविषान्।
विक्रेता मद्यामांसानां स विप्र शूद्र उच्यते ।। 75 ।।

Lakshaadi Tailneelaanaam Kausumbhmadhusavishaan.
Vikreta Maddyamaanasaanaam Sa vipprya Shoodra Uchchyate.

The brahman who sells lac and its products oil indigo plant, flowers' honey, ghee, wine, meat and its product is called a Shudra Brahman (Low Caste Brahman).

देवद्रव्यं गुरुद्रव्यं परदाराभिमर्षणम्।
निर्वाहः सर्वभूतेषु विप्रश्चाण्डाल उच्यते ।। 76 ।।

Devadravyam Gurudravyam Pardaaraabhimarshanam.
Nirvaah Sarvabhooteshu Vipprashchaandaol Uchchyate.

The brahman who steals the things belonging to the Gurus and gods, copulates with other's wife and is able to dewll amongst the beings of any species is called a Pariah-Brahman.

वापीकूपतड़गानामारामसुखेलश्वनाम्।
उच्छेदने निराशंक से विप्रो म्लेच्छ उच्चयते ।। 77 ।।

Vaapeekoopat Daagaanaamaaraamsulcheshvanaam.
Uchchedane Niraashank Se Vippro Mlechcha Uchchyate.

The brahman who recklessly destroys the temples, wells, ponds and orchards without any fear of social repercussion is verily a Mlechha (infidel) Brahman.

परकार्यविहन्ता च दाम्भिकः स्वार्थसाधकः।
छलीद्वेषी सदुक्रूरो मार्जार उच्यते ।। 78 ।।

Parkaaryavihantaa cha daambhikah Svaarthasaadhakaah.
Chaleedveshee Sadukrooro Maarjaar Uchchyate.

The brahman who puts hurdles in other's ways, who is

deceitful, scheming, cruel bearing ill-will for others, sweet by tongue but foul by heart is called a Tom-Cat Brahman.

अर्थाधीताश्च यैर्वेदास्तथा शूद्रान्नभेजिनः।
ते द्विजाः किं करिष्यन्ति निर्विषा इव पन्नगाः ॥ 79 ॥

Arthaadheetaashcha Yairvedaastatha Shooddrannabhojnah.
Te Dvijaah Kim Karishyanti Nirvishaaiva Pannagaah.

The brahman who studies the Veda only for the sake of earning money, who accepts food from the Shudras is verily a snake sans poison. Such brahmans cannot do anything noble.

पीतः क्रुद्धेन तातश्चरणतलहतो वल्लभेऽयेन रोषा
आबाल्याद्विप्रवर्यैः स्ववदनविरे धर्यते वैरिणी मे।
गेहं मे छेदयन्ति प्रतिदिवसममाकान्त पूजानिमित्तात्
तस्मात् खिन्ना सदाहं द्विज कुलनिलय नाथ युक्त
त्यजामि ॥ 80 ॥

Peetah Kruddhen Taatashcharantalahato Vallabhoayen Rosha
Aabhaallyaaddvippravaryaih Svavandanvivare Dhaaryate Vairinee mey.
Gehan mey Chedyanti Pratidivasmamaakaant Poojaanimittat
Tasmaat Khinna sadaaham Dvij Kulnilayam Naath Yuktam Tyajaami.

He who in his rage drank up my sire, the sea; who wrathfully kicked my husband; who from an early childhood bear my enemy Saraswati upon his tongue; who plucks off my lotus to offer them in worshop of Lord Shiva-he or his brethren--the Brahmans--have been bent upon ruining me. Hence I would ever shun going into their houses. [Lakshmi, the Goddess of riches alludes various mythological happenings to Agastya drank up the sea--her father; the sage Bhrigu kicked Lord

Vishnu- -her husband; all the brahmans get their intitiation in learning by chanting the name of Saraswati, the Goddess of speech and her (Lakshmi's) arch enemy; and all the brahmans for the worshop of Lord Shiva, pluck off lotus flowers which abound her home. Hence she would never go to the houses of Brahmans, i.e. the brahmans are hound to-stay poor in wealth because of thisinnate prejudice of the (goodess Lakshmi.)

The Pundit

प्रस्तावसदृशं वाक्यं प्रीवसदृशं प्रियम्।
आत्मशक्तिसमं कोंपं यो जानाति स पण्डितः ।। 81 ।।

Prastaavsadrisham Vaakkyam Prabhaavsadrisham Priyam.
Aatmashaktisamam Kopam Yo Jaanaati Sa Panditah.

He who talks with reference in the context, who knows how to influence people and express his love or anger according to his capacity is called a Pundit. He who knows when and where to speak, how to influence people and how to be wrathful or affectionate in what measure is really a wise man or a Pundit.

The Pariah

दूरादागतं पथिश्रान्तं वृथा च गृहमागतं।
अनर्चयित्वा यो भुंक्ते स वै चाण्डाल उच्चयते ।। 82 ।।

Doordaagatam Pathishraantam Vritha Cha Grihamaagatam.
Anarchyittvaa Yo Bhunkte Sa Vai Chaandaal uchchyate.

He who eats without offering proper respect (food, etc.)

to an unexpected guest, coming from a far off place and bone tired is called a pariah.

तैलाभ्यंगे चिताघूमे मैथुने क्षौर कर्मणि।
तावदभवति चाण्डालो यावत्स्नानं न समाचरेत् ।। 83 ।।

Tailaabhyange Chitaaghoome Maithune Kshauram Karmani.
Taavadbhavati Chaandaalo Yaavattsnaanam Na Samaacharet.

After smearing oil on the body after getting touched by the funera pyre's smoke; after copulation and after getting the hair-nails etc, the man remains pariah till he takes bath.

पक्षिणां काकश्चाण्डाल पशुनां चैव कुक्कुरः।
मुनीनां पापश्चाण्डालः सर्वेषु निनदकः ।। 84 ।।

Paksheenaam Kaakshchaandaal Pashunaam Chaiv Kukkurah.
Muneenaam Paapashchaandaalah Sarveshu Nindakah.

The crow among the birds, the dog among the animals, the sinner among the sages and the back biter among all the being is a pariah.

THE YAVAN

चाण्डालानां सहस्त्रैश्च सूरिभिस्तत्वदर्शिभिः।
एको हि यवनः प्रोक्तो न नीचो यवनात्परः ।। 85 ।।

Chaandaalaanam Sahastraishcha Suribhistattvadarshibhi.
Eko Hi Yavanah Prokto Na Neecho Yavanaattparah.

The learned scholars opine that one Yavan (originally a Greek but commonly understood as any foreigner) is as mean as a thousand pariahs. No one could be meaner than a Yavan.

[Herein Chanakya expresses the deep rooted prejudice prevalent during his times.]

The Guru

गुरुग्निर्द्विजातीनां वर्णानां ब्राह्मणो गुरुः।
पतिरेव गुरुः स्त्रीणां सर्वस्याभ्यगतो गुरुः ।। 86 ।।

Gururagnidirvajaateenaam Varnaanaam Brahmano Guruh.
Patireva Guruh Streenaam Sarvasyaabhyagato Guruh.

(The) fire (god) is the guru of the three social categories viz the brahmans, the kshatriya the warrior class, the vaishya the trader or (merchant class), the brahman is the guru of all the social categories except his own. The guru of woman is her husband and the guest is guru of all the inmates of the house.

[The guru also means the most respectable person besides being the teacher or mentor or perceptor.]

Kuleen (The Scion of a Noble Descent)

एतदर्थं कुलीनानां नृपाः कुर्वन्ति संग्रहम्।
आदिमयावसानेषु न त्यजन्ति च ते नृपम् ।। 87 ।।

Etadarth Kuleenaanaam Nripaah Kurvanti Sangraham.
Aadimaddhyavasaaneshu Na Tyajanti Cha Te Nripam.

The Kuleens or the scions of a noble family never ditch or dupe anybody till their last breath. Hence the kings choose to keep them in their courts.

छिन्नोऽपि चन्दनतरुर्न जहाति गन्ध
वृद्धोऽपि वारणपतिर्न जहाति लीलानम्।
यन्त्रप्रितो मधुरतां न जहार्ति चेक्षु
क्षणोऽपि न ज्यजति शीलगुणान्कुलीनः ।। 88 ।।

Chhinnoapi Chandantarurn Jahaati Gandham
Vriddhoapi Vaaranpatirn Jahaati Leelaanam.
Yantnrpito Madurtaam Na Jahaarti Chekshu
Kshanoapi Na Tyajati Sheelagunaankuleenah.

Even when cut off, the sandal wood-tree doesn't stop giving it's sweet fragrance; even when old the elephant doesn't let go his sturdy plays; even when crushed between the curshers the sugarcane continue; to be sweet--the same way the kuleen, even when fallen on evil days doesn't discard his noble manner and cultured behaviour.

यथा चतुर्भिः कनकं परीक्षयते
निर्घषणच्छेदन तापताड़नैः।
तथा चतुर्भिः पुरुषः परीक्ष्यते
त्यागेन शीलेन गुणेन कर्मणा ।। 89 ।।

Yathaa Chaturbhih Kanakam Pareekshyate
Nirgharshanachedan Taapataadanaih.
Tathaa Chaturbhih Purushah Pareekshyate
Tyaagen Sheelen Guneen Karmanaa.

Like gold is tested by rubbing, cutting, heating and beating so also a man is tested by his sacrifice, moral conduct, innate qualities and his actions.

The Real Beauty

दानेन पाणिर्न तु कंकणेन
स्नानेन शुद्धिर्न तु चन्दनेन।
मानेन तृप्तिर्न तु भोजनेन
ज्ञानेन मुक्तिर्न तु मण्डनेन ॥ 90 ॥

Dannen Paanirn Tu Kankanen
Snaanen Shuddhirna Tu Chandanen.
Maanen Triptirn Tu Bhojanen
Gyaanen Muktirna Tu Mandanen.

Beauty of hands lies in giving alms and not in wearing bracelets; the body becomes clean by taking bath and not by applying sandal wood paste; one feels satisfied by being honoured and not by being fed; one attains to Moksha by knowledge and not by self-decoration

[The last one needs an explanation. Moksha is a stage represented by desirelessness; while the process of self-decoration is the outcome of the attempt to satiate the desires, which is intermiable as the desires have a tendency to grow on what they are fed. Obviously the second stage cannot lead to Moksha, which is the ultimate destination of 'the conscious-soul']

The Real Friend

उत्सवे व्यसने प्राप्ते दुर्भिक्षे शत्रुसंकटे।
राजद्वारे श्मशाने च यस्तिष्ठति स बान्धवः ।। 91 ।।

Uttsave Vyasane Praapte Durbhikshe Shatrusnkate.
Raajdvaare Shmashaane Cha Yastishthati Sa Baandhavah.

He who is together with you in festivities, distress, drought, and in the crisis caused by an enemy attack, in the royal courts and in the crematorium is your real friend.

विद्या मित्रां प्रवासेषु भार्या मित्रां गृहेषु च।
व्याध्तिस्यौषधिं मित्रां धर्मो मित्रां मृतस्य च ।। 92 ।।

Vidhya Mitram Pravaaseshu Bhaaryaa Mitram Grahesh Cha.
Vyaadhitasyaushadham Mitram Dharmo Mitram Mritasya Cha.

Away from home, in the foreign strand, one's knowledge is one's best friend, inside home one's wife is one's best friend. For a patient the first friend is efficacious medicine while after death one's Dharma is one's best friend.

[It is believed that he who is adhered to his Dharma religiously and firmly gets the divine rewards after death.]

Pleasures and Happiness

यस्य पुत्रो वशीभूतो भार्या छन्दानुगामिनी।
विभवे यस्य सन्तुष्टिस्तस्य स्वर्ग इहैव हि ।। 93 ।।

Yasya Putro Vasheebhooto Bharyaa Chandaarugaamini.

Vibhave Yasya Santushtistastya Svarga ihaiv Hi.

If one has obedient son, a pious wife following the Vedic path and if one is satisfied with his material possessions, one is living verily in the heaven.

भोज्यं भोजनशक्तिश्चं रतिशक्तिश्चं वारांगना।
विभवो दानशक्तिश्च नाल्पस्य तपसः फलम् ।। 94 ।।

Bhojjyam Bhojanshaktishacham Ratishaktishcham Vaaraanganaa.
Vibhao Daanshaktishcha Naalpasya Tapasah Phalam.

Getting good food alongwith the power to digest it, getting beautiful woman alongwith the power to enjoy her, getting rich alongwith the capability to dole out elms--are the outcome of one's no less arduous penance and austerities.

सन्तोषामृततृप्तानां यत्सुखं शान्तिरेव चे।
नच तद्धनलुब्धनामितश्चेतश्च धवताम् ।। 95 ।।

Santoshaamrittriptaanaam Yattsukham Shaantireva Cha.
Na Cha Taddhanlubddhaanaamitashchetashch Dhaavatam.

The nectar of satisfaction begetting peace and happiness cannot available for the people hankering after material riches and physic pleasures.

नास्ति कामसमो व्याधिर्नास्ति मोहसमो रिपुः।
नास्ति कोप समो वह्नि र्नास्ति ज्ञानात्परं सुखम् ।। 96

Naasti Kaamasamo Vyaadhirnaasti Mohasamo Ripuh.
Naasti Kopasamo Vahanirnaasti Gyaanaatparam Sukham.

Uncontrollable sexual craving is the most deadly disease, ignorance and infatuation are the most deadly foes, wrath is the most deadly fire and knowledge of the self is the happiness supreme.

माता चकमला देवी पिता देवो जनार्दनः।
बान्ध्वा विष्णुभाक्ताश्चस्वदेशो भूवनत्रायम् ।। 97 ।।

Maataa Cha Kamallaa Devi Pitaa Devo Janaardanah.
Baandhavaa Vishnubhakttaashcha Svadesho Bhuvantrayam.

He who has his mother like the Goddess Laksmi, father like Lord Vishnu and brothers and other close relations like devotees of Lord Vishnu dwells in a house replete with all the pleasures of the three realms (the heaven, the earth and the nether world of Patal-lok).

GRIEF

कान्तावियोग स्वजनापमानो
ऋणस्य शेषः कुनृपष्य सेवा।
दरिद्रभावो विषया सभा च
विनाग्निमेते प्रदहन्ति कायम् ।। 98 ।।

Kaantaaviyog Suajanaapmaano
Rinasyaasheshah Kunripasya Sevaa.
Dariddra Bhaavo Vishyaa Sabhaa Cha
Vinaagnimete Pradahanti Kaayam.

Separation from the beloved, insult by the close relations, unpaid debt, service to a wicked king poverty and association of the crooked persons incinerate the body even without fire.

कुग्रामवासः कुलहीन सेवा
कुभोजनं क्रोधमुखी च भार्या।
पुत्राश्च मूर्खो विधवा च कन्या
विनाग्निमेते प्रदहन्ति कायम् ।। 99 ।।

Kugraamvaasah Kulheen Sevaa
Kubhojanam Krodhamukhee cha Bhaaryaa.
Putrashcha Moorkho Vidhavaa Cha Kanyaa
Vinaagnimete Pradahanti Kaayam.

Residence in the village of wicked persons, service to lowly family, unnourishing food, foul speaking wife, foolish sons, widowed daughter – all these incinerate the body even without fire.

वृद्धकाले मृता भार्या बन्धुहस्तगतं धनम्।
भोजनं च पराधीनं तिस्त्र पुसां विडम्बना ।। 100 ।।

Vriddhakaale Mritaa Bhaaryaa Bandhuhastagatam Dhanam.
Bhojanam Cha Paraadheenam Tishtrapusaam Vidambanaa.

Death of wife in the old age, money under brother's control and the dependence on others for daily bread cause a great anamoly, hence grief in one's life.

कष्टं च खलु मूर्खत्वं कष्टं खलु यौवनम्।
कष्टात्कष्टरं चैव परगेहनिवासनम् ।। 101 ।।

Kashtam Cha Khalu Moorkhattvam Kashtam Cha Khalu Yauvanam.
Kashtaattkashtakaram Chaiv Pargehenivaaasaham.

Although the foolishness (of the self) and (insurmountable) youthful exuberance cause grief yet the greatest grief is caused by one's (forced) stay at other's house.

अयमममृतणनिधनं नायको औषधीनां
अमृतमयशरीरः कान्तियुक्तोऽपि चन्द्राः।
भवति विगतरश्मिर्मण्डले प्राप्य भानोः
परसदननिविष्टः को न लघुत्वं याति ।। 102 ।।

Ayamamritnanidhaanam Naayako Aushadheenaam
Amritmaya Shareerah Kaantiyuktoapi Chandrah.
Bhavati Vigatarashmirmandale Praappya Bhaanoh
Parsadananivishtah Kona Laghuttvam Yaati.

This fount of vitality, the lord of all medicines, this moon with the body made of nectar and the shine enchanting, grows how splendourless the moment it arrives in the halo of the sun. Who doesn't lose stature by stepping in other's house ?

[it is believed that all herbs and vegetation – the source of medicine –derive their efficacious potency from the rays of the moon which is said to be made of nectar. Despite its all natural splendour and gifts even the moon loses its charm the moment the sun rises i.e., the moment it survives beyond darkness and tries to enter the house of the sun that is the day-time.]

अनवस्थिकायस्य न जने न वने सुखम्।
जनो दहति संसदर्गाद् वनं सगविवर्जनात ।। 103।।

Anavasthikayasya na Jana na vane sukham
Jano Dhati Sansadargaad Vanam Sagavivarjanaat.

He whose mind is not steady doesn't get happiness either amongst the people or in the loneliness of the jungle. When lonely he longs for company and when in company he yearns for loneliness.

संसारातपदग्धनां त्रायो विरान्तिहेतवः।
अपत्यं च कलत्रां च सतां संगतिरेव च ।। 104 ।।

Sansaaraatpadaghaanam Trayo Vishraantihetavah.
Apattyam Cha Kaltram Cha Sataam Sangatirev Cha.

Those who are signed by the mundane fare get solace only under three conditions staying with the son, with the wife or in the company of the noble person.

[It means a persons tired and dwadled by the mundane duties gets solace in the company of his family or of the noble gentle persons. Such a company rejuvenates his exhausted physique and over worked mind.]

Knowledge or Education

रुपयौवनसम्पना विशालकुलसंभवाः।
विद्याहीना न शोभन्ते निर्गन्ध इव किंशुकाः ।। 105 ।।

Roopyauvahsampanna Vishaatkulsambhavah.
Viddyaaheena Na Shobhante Nirgandhaa Iv Kinshukaah.

Despite having a well endowed physique; beauty charms and belonging to a high and big family if a man is uneducated or ignorant, he looks as useless and unimpressive as the kinshuk (palaash) flowers having only colour but no fragrance.

कामधेनुगुणा विद्या ह्ययकाले पफलदायिनी।
प्रवासे भातृसद्दशा विद्या गुप्तं धनं स्मृतम् ।। 106 ।।

Kamdhenugunaa Viddyaa Hayakaale Phaladaayani.
Pravaase Bhaatrisadrisha Viddyaa Guptam Dhanam Smritam.

Knowledge (or education) is like the cow of plenty, giving good things even in the most adverse period in the foreign strands;it protects like mother and renders help as though it is a veritable secret treasure.

श्वानपुच्छमिव व्यर्थ जीवितं विद्यया बिना।
न गृह्यं गोपने शक्तं न च दंशनिवारणे ।। 107 ।।

Shvaanpuchchamiv Vyarth Jeevitam Viddyayaa Binaa.
Na Griham Gopane Shaktam Na Cha Darshanivaarne.

An illiterate person's life is as useless as the tail of a dog neither capable of covering its privities nor in warding off the flies and mosquitoes. [Chanakya says that without education or knowledge life has no value. Neither it can take out the wants nor it can provide comfort to the unfortunate man.]

विद्वान् प्रशस्यते लोके विद्वान् सर्वत्रा गौरवम्।
विद्यया लभते सर्व विद्या सर्वत्रा पूज्यते ।। 108 ।।

Viddvaan Prashaste Loke Viddvaan Sarvatra Gauravam.
Viddyayaa Labhate Sarva Viddyaa Sarvatra Poojyate.

An educated man – a scholar gets accolades from all and earn reputation in the society. Since education helps to one get everything on desires in life, it is adored everywhere.

द्गतो न सचरित खे न चलेच्च वार्ता
पूर्व न जलिपतामिंद न च संगमोऽस्ति।
व्योम्निसिंम रविशशिग्रहणं प्रशस्तं
जानाति यो द्विजवरः स कर्थ न विद्वान् ।। 109 ।।

Dooto Na Sancharit Khe na Challechch Vaartaa
Poorvam Na Jalpitmidam Na Cha Sangamoasti.
Vyomnismim Ravipshashigrahanam Prashstam
Janati Yo Dvijavarah Sa Katham Na Viddvan.

Neither a messenger could be sent to the sky not any communication could be established nor anyone told us about anyone existing there, still the scholars predict with great precision about the Solar and Lunar eclipses. Who would hesitate in calling them the very erudite scholars?

STUDENTS

सुखार्थी चेत् त्येजेद्विद्यां विद्यार्थी चेत् त्यजेत्यसुखम्।
सुखार्थिनः कुतो विद्या कुतो विद्यार्थिनः सुखम् ।। 110 ।।

Sukhaarthee Chet Tyejedviddyaam Viddyaarthee Chet Tyajettsukam.
Sukhaartheenah Kuto Viddyaa Kuto Viddyaarthinah Sukham.

If one craves for comfort, then he should drop the idea of studying and if one wants to study sincerely then he should stop craving for comfort. One cannot get comfort and education simultaneously.

कामं क्रोधं तथा लोभं स्वाद श्रृंगाकौतुकम्।
अतिनिद्राऽतिसेवा च विद्यार्थी ह्याष्ट वर्जयेत् ।। 111 ।।

Kaamam Krodham tathaa Lobham Svaad Shringaarkautukam.
Atinidraatisevaa cha Viddyaarthee Hayaashta Varjayet.

A student desirous of getting education must shun the following right activities— sexual intercourse, gratification of the tongue, showing anger and greed, caring for personal beautification, moving about the fair and fate for entertainment, excessive sleeping and indulging in anything excessively.

[In short Chanakya says that for getting education the student must perform a rigorous penance complete with all the severe austerities. He who tries to get education in comfort fails to get it in reality and vice versa.]

यथा खनित्व खनित्रोण भूतले वारि विन्दति।
तथा गुरुगतां विद्यां शुश्रूषुरधिगच्छति ।। 112 ।।

Yathaa Khanittvaa Khanitren Bhootale Vaari Vindati.
Tathaa Gurugataam Viddyaam Shushrushuradhigachhati.

Like one digs the ground deep by a mattock to bring out water, so should a student attempt to get knowledge from one's Guru.

[One has to toil very hard to get water from the depth of earth. Chanakya says that the same way a student should toil and render strenuous service to his Guru to get knowledge from him.]

एकाक्षरं प्रदातारं यो गुरुं नाभिवन्दते।
श्वानयोनि शतं भुक्तवा चाण्डालेष्वभिजायते ।। 113 ।।

Ekaaksharam Pradaataaram Yo guruam Naabhivandate.
Shvaanyoni Shatam Bhuktavaa Chaandaaleshvabhijaayate.

He who doesn't pay obeisance to his Guru even after receiving the knowledge of the Ekakshar Mantra (the mono syllable 'OM') gets hundred births in the dog's species and then becomes a pariah in human life.

पुस्तकं प्रत्याधीतं नाधीतं गुरुसन्निधौ।
सभामध्ये न शोभन्ते जारगर्भा इव स्त्रिाय: ।। 114 ।।

Pustakam Prattyaadheetam Naadheetam Gurusannidhau.
Sabhamaddhye Na Shobhante Jaargarbhaiv Istriyah.

He who tries to get knowledge only by reading books and not through the grace of a Guru deserves the position in a society due only to a woman impregnated through an illegal relationship.

[A strong upholder of the Guru-Shishya tradition, Chanakya considers that to be no knowledge at all which is received without the Guru's teaching. He asserts, and very rightly so, that such a knowledge would be incomplete and hence damaging.]

कि कुलेन विशालेन विद्याहीने च देहिनाम्। दुष्कुलं चाऽपि विदुषो देवैरपि हि पूज्यते ।। 115 ।।

Kim Kulen Vishaalen Viddyaaheene Cha Dehinaam.
Duskulam Chapi Vidusho Devarirapi Hi Poojyate.

An uneducated person is wrothless even if he might be belonging to a renowned family. A scholar, despite belonging to a low rated family, is adored by even the gods.

धनहीनो न च हीनश्च धनिक स सुनिश्चयः। विद्या रत्नेन हीनो यः स हीनः सर्ववस्तुषुः ।। 116 ।।

Dhanheeno na Cha heenashcha Dhanik sa Sunishchayah.
Viddhya Ratnen Heeno Yah Sa Heenah Sarvavstushuh.

A man devoid of wealth is in fact not a poor man. He might become wealthy. But one who is uneducated is actually a pauper in all aspects.

एकमेवाक्षरं यस्तुः गुरुः शिष्टां प्रबोधयेत्। पृथिव्यां नास्ति तद्द्रव्यं यद् दत्त्वा दानृणे भवेत् ।। 117 ।।

Ekamevaaksharam Yastuh Guruh Shishtaam Prabodhayet.
Prithivyaam Naasti Taddravyam Yad Daatvaa Daanrino Bhavet.

The Guru who enlightens (his pupils) by mono-syllable Mantra ('OM') obliges (them) so deeply that nothing on earth can repay this obligation to him.

[The pupils who receive such education from their Guru can never undebt themselves.

Worship of the Virtue

गुणा: सर्वत्र पूज्यन्ते न महत्योऽपि सम्पद: ।
पूर्णेन्दु कि तथा वन्द्यो निष्कलंको यथा कुश: ।। 118 ।।

Gunaah Sarvatra Poojyante Na Mahattyoapi Sampadah.
Poornendu Kim Tathaa Vanddyo Nishkalenko Yatha Kushah.

It is virtue, which is adored everywhere and not the riches or even excess of them. Does the full moon is accorded the same respect as given to the weaker moon ?

[Chanakya impliedly says that the initial phase of the moon, specifically the moon of the second day is accorded greater regard because the stains of the moon are not visible at this stage, which the full moon, despite being more luminous, has its stains clearly defined. It is only the blemishless part of the moon that is accorded the greater respect. Similarly, a rich-man with huge property would not command greater respect, if he is not virtuous or free from blemish, than the person having much less money or riches but more virtuous and untainted by any blemish.]

विवेकिनमनुप्राप्तो गुणो याति मनोज्ञताम्।
सुतरां रत्नमाभाति चामीकरनियोजितम्।। 119 ।।

Vivekinmunuprapato Guno Yaati Manogyataam.
Sutaraam Rattnamaabhaati Chaameekarniyojitam.

Virtues gleam more when these are in a wise person like a gem adding to the beauty when embedded in gold.

गुणं सर्वत्रा तुल्योऽपि सीदत्येको निराश्रय:।
अनर्यमपि मणिक्यं हेमारयमपेक्षते ।। 120 ।।

Gunam Sarvatra Tullyoapi Seedttyeko Niraashrayah.
Anadharyamapi Maanikkyam Hemaashrayamapekshate,

If left without a proper support, even the virtuous gets distressed. However blemishless be a gem, it needs a base to shine from.

सत्यं माता पिता ज्ञानं धर्मो भ्राता दया सखा।
शान्ति: पत्नी क्षमा पुत्रा: षडेते मम बान्ध्वा: ।। 121 ।।

Sattyani Maataa Pitaa Gyaanam Dharmo Bhraataa Dayaa Sakhaa.
Shaantih Pattni Kshmaa Putrah Shatete Mam Bandhavaah.

Truth is my mother, knowledge is father, my Dharma is my brother, compassion my friend, peace is my wife and forgiveness is my son. These six virtues are my real relations, the rest are all false!

व्यालाश्रयापि विपफलापि सकण्टकापि
वक्रापि पंकसहितापि दुरासदापि।
गन्धेन बन्धुरसि केतकि सर्वजन्तो-रेको
गुण: खलु निहन्ति समस्तदोषान् ।। 122 ।।

Vyaalaashrayaapi Viphalaapi Sakantkaapi
Vakraapi Pankasahitaapi Duraasadaapi.
Gandhen Bandhurasi Ketaki Sarvajantoreko
Gunah Khalu Nihanti Samastdoshaan.

O Ketaki (pandanus)! Inspite of your being the dwelling place of the snakes, your being a fruitless– full of thorns–shurb originating in the mud and accessible with great difficulty, still you are dear to all because of your sweet fragrance. Most certainly one good virtue haloes every other defect.

गुणैरुत्तमतां यान्ति नोच्चैरासनसंस्थितै:।
प्रासादशिखरस्थोपि किं काको गरुडायते ।। 123 ।।

Gunairuttamattaam Yaanti Nochairaasansansthitai.
Praasaadshikharasthoapi Kim Kaako Garudaayate.

It is virtues, which enhance one's stature and not the high position. Even if perched atop a royal palace, a crow cannot become Garur (the acquila bird of mythological origin, believed to be the lord of the birds).

परमोक्तगुणो यस्तु निर्गुणोऽपि गुणी भवेत्।
इन्द्रोऽपि लघुतां याति स्वयं प्रख्यापितैर्गुणै: ।। 124 ।।

Paramoktaguno Yastu Nirgunoapi Gunee Bhavet.
Indroapi Laghutaam Yaati Svayam Prakhyaapitaairgunaih.

If others praise even the virtueless person, he may acquire some status, but even if Indra (the lord of the gods) starts praising his own virtues he will be little his stature.

Wisdom

यस्य नास्ति स्वयं प्रज्ञा शास्त्रां तस्य करोति किम्।
लोचनाभ्यां विहीनस्य दर्पणं किं करिष्यति ।। 125 ।।

Yasya Naasti Svayam Pragyaa Shaastram Tassya Karoti Kim.
Lochanaabhyaam Viheenasya Darpanam Kim Karishyati.

What can all the scriptures do for a person devoid of his own wisdom? What use has a mirror for a blind man?

अन्त:सारविहीननामुपदेशो न जायते।
मलयाचलसंसर्पात्र वेणुश्चन्दनायते ।। 126 ।।

Antahsaarviheenanaamupdesho na Jaayate.
Malyaachal Sansarpaanna Venushchandanaayate.

All sermons are wasted on a person devoid of wisdom. Even if grown in the Malayaachal (the area abounding with sandal trees) the bamboo cannot become the sandalwood!

न वेत्तियो यस्य गुणप्रकर्ष
स तु सदा निन्दंति नात्रा चित्राम्।
यथा किराती करिकुम्भलब्धं
मुक्तां परित्यज्य विभर्ति गुञ्जाम् ।। 127 ।।

Na vetti Yo Yassya Gunaprakarsha
Sa tu sadaa Nindanti Naatra Chittram.
Yatha Kiraati Karikumbhalabdhaam
Muktaam Parittyaajya Vibharti Gunchaam.

No wonder if anyone not aware of certain virtues derides them. Kirati (the Bhil woman) would happily discard the pearls found in elephants' head for the Gunjas (the common, cheap beads) and wear them in the necklace.

[Since the Bhil woman is not aware of the high value of pearls found in the elephants' head, she rejects them for the common beads.]

दानार्थिनो मधुकरा यदि कर्णताले
तस्यैव गण्डयुगमण्डनहानिरेव
भृंगाः पुनर्विकचपद्मवने वसन्ति ।। 128 ।।

Daanaarthino Madhukaraa Yadi Kana taalai
Doorikritaa Kanivaren Madaandbuddhayaa.
Tasyaiv Gandayugamandanahaanireva
Bhirgaah Punarvikachapaddmavane Vasanti.

Blinded by his intoxication, the elephant sent away the

Bhanwars (Black-bees), warding them off by the movement of his ears. The loss was not of the Bhanwars but of the elephant as his visage lost the charm. The Bhanwars went back to the cluster of lotus flowers.

[The young elephants have their ears discharge a sweet smelling substance, which attracts the black-bees. The herd of black-bees around the elephant's head add to the charm of the pachyderm's face. When he shoos them away by fluttering his ears, it is the elephant that loses his charms not the bees, which go back to the cluster of lotus flowers. Meaning thereby that if the fools do not give respect to the virtues, it is they who suffer the loss not the virtues, which have many admirers.]

पठन्ति चतुरो वेदान् धर्मशास्त्राण्यनेकशः।
आत्मानं नैव जानन्ति दर्वीं पाकरसं यथा ।। 129 ।।

Pathanti Chaturo Vedaan Dharmashastraannyanekashah.
Aattmaanam Naiv Jaananti Daveem Paakarasam Yathaa.

Even if a fool reads the four Vedas and other scriptures but he cannot realise the self like the ladle, repeatedly entering the food, fails to discern the taste of the food.

Great Man

अधीत्येदं यथाशास्त्रं नरो जानाति सत्तमः।
धर्मोपदेशविख्यातं कार्याकार्यशुभाशुभम् ।। 130 ।।

Adheettyedam Yathaashaastram Naro Jaanaati Sattamah.
Dharmopadeshvikhyaatam Kaaryaaa Kaayashubhashubham.

He is really a great man who derives the real meaning after

reading these aphorisms (collection of the pithy sayings on morality) detailing what one should and what one shouldn't do; what is Dharma and what is not; and what is auspicious and what is not.

> अहो स्वित् विचित्राणि चरितानि महात्मनाम्।
> लक्ष्मीं तृणाय मनयन्ते तद्भरेण नमन्ति च ।। 131 ।।

Aho Svit Vichitraani Charitaani Mahaattmanaam.
Laxammem Trinaaya Mannyante Taddbharen Namanti cha.

All the great men have a typical character. Though they deem the Goddess Lakshmi (riches) as though she is a mere straw but they get suppressed by her weight.

[Chanakya says that the great men do not attach much importance to the riches but as they grow rich, they become more and more submissive and humble.]

> स्वगस्थितानामिह जीवलोके
> चत्वारि चिह्नानि वसन्ति देहे।
> दानप्रसंगो मधुरा च वाणी
> देवार्चनं ब्राह्मणतर्पणं च ।। 132 ।।

Svargamsthitaanaamih Jeevaloke
Chattvaari Chinnhaaani VAsanti Dehe.
Daanprasango Madhura Cha Vaani
Devaarchanam Braahamantarpanam cha.

He who has sweet voice, who worships the gods and keeps the brahmans satisfied and who takes interest in giving alms is actually a divine soul in this mundane realm. He is a great man who has all these four qualities.

युगान्ते प्रचलेन्मेरुः कल्पान्ते सप्त सागराः।
साध्वः प्रतिपन्नार्थन्न चलन्ति कदाचन ।। 133 ।।

Yugaante Prachalenmeruch Kalpaanted Sapta Saagaraah.
Saadhavah Pratipannarthaanna Chalanti Kadaanchan.

The sumeru Mountain may be displaced from its position at the end of an epoch or all the seven seas may be disturbed at the end of a Kalp [a very big unit of time containing twenty seven cycles of the epochs (yugs), each containing four yugas : Satya, Treta, Dwapar and Kaliyug] but the great noble men never waver from their chosen path.

अयुक्तस्वामिनो युक्तं युक्तं नीचस्य दूषणम्।
अमृतं राहवे मृत्युर्विषं शंकभूषणम् ।। 134 ।।

Ayiktasvaamino Yuktam Yuktam Neechasya Dooshanam.
Amritam Raahave Mrittyurisham Shanker bhooshanam.

Getting an able owner even the worthless thing becomes useful and adorable while a worthless owner ruins the value of a priceless thing. Lord Shankar made even the deadly poison an ornament of his throat while Rahu, the demon got beheaded even when he had sipped nectar.

[Chanakya alludes two mythological events to bring home his Point, At the time of that "Mighty Churning of the Seas" by the demons and the gods, when deadly poison surfaced, for the welfare of entire creation, Lord Shankar drank it but didn't let it go down the throat which turned blue by the excessive toxicity of the poison. But even that poison earned him an epithet the 'blue-throated' or the 'Neelkantha'. When nectar surfaced by that Churning, the gods and the demons began to fight for it. Then Lord Vishnu assumed the form of a beautiful woman 'Mohini' and began to pour it down the throat of the gods. Seeing through the game of Lord Vishnu, one of the demons, Rahu jumped to the side of the gods, in disguise, to receive nectar. But the moment he took a sip of that divine (ion, the sun-god and the moon god exposed him and Lord Vishnu there and then beheaded him by his Chakra (disc). But since he had chit- in his throat, he couldn't be dead despite his head being hacked off. Since then, it is belived mythologically that the head is surviving separately as Rahu and his trunk as Ketu.]

अधमा ध्नमिच्छछन्ति धनं मानं च मयमा: I
उत्तमा मानमिच्छन्ति मानो हि महतां धनम् II 135 II

Adhamaa Dhanamichanti Dhanam Maanan cha Maddhyamaah Uttamaa.
Maanamichanti Maano Hi Mahataam Dhanam.

The mean aspire only for wealth, the mediocre yearn for wealth and honour both while the nobles care only for honour. The real treasure of great men is only honour.

प्राप्त द्रूयतप्रसंगेन मयो स्त्रीप्रसंगत: I
रात्रौ चौरप्रसंगेन कालो गच्छति धीमताम् II 136 II

Praapta Dhyutprasangen Madhyaahne Streeprasangatah.
Ratrau Chaurprasangen Kalo Gachhati Dheetaam.

The greatmen-scholars pass their mornings in gambling, afternoon with women and nights with thieves. This is how they pass their time.

[Chanakya's intelligent allusion provide great sense in this otherwise and apparently-atrocious observation. Speaking epigrammatically, he hints that the great men pass their mornings in reading the Mahabharat which resulted out of the gambling addiction of Yundhisthar. The Mahabharata highlights the general weakness of human Characters. So the great scholars first concentrate on human follies to guard against them. In the afternoon they study the Ramayana which tells them about the dreadful consequences of the infatuation to a woman--Ravan's falling for Sita and ultimately meeting his sorry end. In the nights they read about the Lord Krishna who is affectionately called the head of the thieves as he used to steal butter and milk and also the hearts of the Gopis. Chanakya says that the great men never waste their time and study these epics to derive lessons from them and mend their ways accordingly. They always are in the pursuit of knowledge.]

Good Company

दर्शनयानसंस्पर्शैर्मत्स्यी कूर्मी च पक्षिणी।
शिशु पालायते नित्यं तथा सज्जनसंगतिः ।। 137 ।।

Darshandhyansanspasheimartsyee Koormee Cha Pakshini.
Shishu Paalaayate Nittyam Tathaa Sajjan Sangatih.

Like fish, tortoise and bird rear up their infants by looking, caring and touching them respectively, so does good company with respect to human beings.

साधुम्यस्ते निवर्तन्ते पुत्राः मित्राणि बांध्वाः।
ये च तैः सह गन्तारस्तद्धर्मात्सुकृतं कुलम! ।। 138 ।।

Saadhubhyaste Nivartante Putrah Mitraani Baandhavah.
Ye cha tain Saha Ganttaarstaddhramaattsukritam Kulam.

Normally sons, friends and brothers have a tendency to take one away from the company of holymen and noble, scholarly persons. But still those who are able to maintain such contact bring piety in the family atmosphere.

संसार कूट वृक्षस्य द्वे पफले ह्यमृतोपमे।
सुभाषितं च सुस्वादुः संगति सज्जने जने ।। 139 ।।

Sansaar Koot Vrishassya Duephale Hyumritopame.
Subhaashitam Cha Susvaauh Sangati Sajjane Jane.

This world, in the form of a tree, has two nectareous fruits :

sweet speech and good company.

साधूनां दर्शनं पुण्यं तीर्थभूता: हि साधव:।
कालेन पफलते तीर्थ: सद्य: साधु समागम: ।। 140 ।।

Saadhoonaam Darshanam Punnyam Teerthabhoothaah Hi Saadhavah.
Kaalen Phalate Teerthah Saddyah Saadhu Samaagamah.

One earns great merit by meeting the holymen who are like the sacred places with the difference that their meeting gives immediate good result while the visit to sacred places gives it after some time.

सत्सगतेर्भवति हि साधुता खलानां
साधूनां न हि खलसंगते: खलत्वम्।
आमोद कुसुमभवं भूदेव धत्ते
मृद्रन्धं न हिकुसुमानिक धरयन्ति ।। 141 ।।

Satsangaterbhavati Hi Saadhutaa Khalaanaam
Sadhunaan Nahi Kalsangeteh Khattvam.
Aamodam Kusumbhavam Bhoodev Dhatte
Mrindagandham Nahi Kussumaani Dhaarayanti.

A good company generates the noble elements in the nature of the wicked but a bad or wicked company does not generate wickedness in the noble person. It is only the soil, which accepts the fragrance of flowers and not the fragrance, which refuses to accept the odour of the soil.

गम्यते यदि मृगेन्द्रमन्दिरे
लभ्यते करिकपोलमौक्तिकम्।
जम्बुका रयगतं च प्राप्यते
वत्सपुच्छखरचर्मखण्डम् ।। 142 ।।

Gammyate Yadi Mrigendramandire
Labbhyate Krikapolmauktikam.
Jambukaashrayagatam cha prappyate
Vattsapuchakharcharmakhandam.

If any one goes to the den of a lion, one might get the pearl of the elephant's head. But a visit to the lair of a jackal would yield only the tail-piece of a calf or the bits of donkey's skin.

[Meaning that high company yields noble benefits and the poor association gives only inferior things.]

आपदर्थ धनं रक्षेच्छयश्च किमापदः।
कदाचिच्चलिता लक्ष्मी संचितोऽपि विनश्यति ।। 143 ।।

Aapadartham Dhanam Rakshechayashcha Kimaapadah.
Kadaachichachalitaa Laxmi Sanditaapi Vinashyati.

One must save money for the evil days. It is not that the distress won't touch the rich people. Riches are by nature fickle and even the large, accumulated wealth can be destroyed in a trice.

मूर्खाः यत्रा न पूज्यन्ते धन्यं यत्रा सुसंचितम्।
दाम्पत्योः कलहो नास्ति तत्रा श्री स्वयमागता ।। 144 ।।

Moorkhah Yatra Na Poojyante Dhaannyam Yatra Susanchitam.
Daampattyoh Kalaho Naasti Tatra Shree Suayamaagataa.

Where the dunces are not honoured, where the eatables are available in abundance, where the husband and wife do not quarrel with each other – the Goddess Lakshmi (or good luck) comes in that house on her own.

यस्यार्थस्तस्यमित्राणि यस्यार्थस्तस्य बांधवा:।
यस्यार्थ: स पुमांल्लोके यस्यार्थ: स च पण्डित: ।। 145 ।।

Yassyaarthsstrassyamittraani Yassyaarthasstasya Baandhavah.
Yassyarthah Sa Puamaamlloke Yassyaarthah Sa cha panditah.

He who has money has many friends, many relations and he is also deemed a great man and a scholar.

[Chanakya's this aphorism is in direct contradiction with his earlier saying in which he asserts that a great man is he who doesn't care for money but for honour. May be he is trying to compare what ought to be with what is in the reality.]

उपर्जितानां वित्तानां त्याग एव हि रक्षणम्।
तड़ागोदरसंस्थानां परिवाह इवाम्मसाम् ।। 146 ।।

Upaarjitaanaam vittaanaam Tyaag Evahi Rakshanam.
Taddagodarsansthaanaam Parivaah Ivaammasaam.

Like it is essential for the bound water to have a little flow for its purity, so it is necessary to donate the part of the earned wealth for its protection.

वित्तं देहि गुणान्वितेषु मतिमाननान्यत्रा देहि क्वचित्
प्राप्तं वारितिधेर्जलं ध्नयुचां माधुर्ययुक्तं सदा।
जीवा: स्थावर जंगमाश्च सकला सजीव्य भूमण्डलं
भूय: पश्य तदैव कोटिगुणितं गच्छन्त्यम्भोनिधिम् ।। 147 ।।

Vittam Dehi gunaaniviteshu Matimaannaannyatra Dehi Kvachit
Praaptam Vaaritidherjalam Dhanyachaam Maadhuryayuktam Sadaa.
Jeevaah Sthaavar Jangamaashcha Sakalaa Sajeevya Bhoomadalam
Bhooyah Pashya Tadaiv Kotigunitam Gachaanttyammbhonidhim.

O wise! Give riches to the virtuous only, never to the undeserving, to those who lack good qualities. The clouds derive water from the seas and then making it sweet and then rain on the earth to make the beings of the earth survive. Then this water returns to the sea many million times more than the water the seas had given to the clouds.

[Chanakya says that if one gives money to someone who is wise, intelligent and full of virtues, the receiver is able to multiply it many times over and this way not only the receiver but the whole society is benefited. Giving the analogy of the sea-water-cloudrain- sea cycle, he explains his point very cogently. If the seas give water to cloud (the virtuous, deserving receiver), it makes it sweet and then rains it over the earth to help all beings survive there. Then through rivers this rain water, multiplied million times over by the clouds, returns to the seas, and during the process keeping the earth lush and green and its beings rejuvenated.

किं तया क्रियते लक्ष्म्या या वधूरिव केवला।
या तु वेश्यैव सामान्यपथिकैरिपि भुज्यते ।। 148 ।।

Kimtayaa Kriyate Laxammyaa Yaa Vadhooriv Kevalaa.
Yaa Tu Veshyaiv Saamaanmyapathikairapi Bhujjyate.

What are the uses of the riches kept inside the house like the bride of an orthodox and traditional family? And those riches which like the prostitutes are enjoyed by all have no usefulness either.

[The miser keeps his wealth secretly hidden in the vaults which serve no purpose of the society. And the riches with the fools are like the prostitute enjoyed by others, especially the low category people. In that case also the wealth is not well spent. This way, obliquely Chanakya says that riches should be spent in the welfare of the virtuous who help the society and they should neither be amassed in a miserly way nor spent extravagantly.]

कुचैलिनं दन्तमलोपधरिणं
ब्रशिनं निष्ठुरभाषितं च।
सूर्योदये चास्तमिते शयानं
विमुचतेश्रीर्यदि चक्राणि: ।। 149 ।।

Kuchailinam Dantamalopdharrinim
Bahvaashinam Nishthar Bhaashitam cha.
Sooryodaye Chaastamite Shayaanam
Vimunchateshreeryadi Chakraanih.

All the riches and prosperity shun those person including even Lord Vishnu if he is also one of those who wear dirty clothes; who have filthy teeth; who are glutton; who speak harsh language and who continue to sleep even after the sun rise.

[Chanakya says that callous lazy persons never come in wealth. Even if they happen to receive wealth by chance, it won't stay with them if they continue to be callous and lazy. To be rich and prosperous one must be active and clean.]

अतिक्लेशेन ये चार्थाः धर्मस्यातिक्रमेण तु।
शत्रुणां प्राणिपातेन ते ते ह्यर्थः न भवन्तु मे ।। 150।।

Atikleshen Ye Chaarthaah Dharmasyaati Kramentu.
Shatroonaam Pranipaaten Te Hyaarthah Na Bhavantu Me.

I don't crave for such a wealth which is extorted by saddening someone, by irreligious and immoral means or by seeking shelter of the enemies.

[In the mordem context this could be interpreted as an unwillingness to get such a wealth as may be received by immoral means, by torturing anyone or from the enemy of one's faith or country, i.e. the blackmoney or the money received through the smuggling activities or through the treacherous deal with the enemies.]

अपुत्रास्य गृह शूनयं दिशः शून्यास्तवबान्ध्वाः।
मूर्खस्य हृदयं शून्यं सर्वशून्यं दरिद्रता ।। 151 ।।

Aputrasya Griha Shoonnyam Dishah Shoonnyaasttvabaandhavaah.
Moorkhassya Hridayam Shoonnyam Sarvashoonmyam Daridrataa.

A home is vacuous for the one who has lost his son (or who has no son); all the quarters of the world are vacuous for him who has lost a brother (or who has no brothers); for the fool his heart is vacuous (i.e., he has no plans, no occupation) but for the pauper everything is meaningless or vacuous.

[Here the vacuousness should be deemed to be absence of any hope. Obviously, a home has no hope for the sonless person; for the brotherless person, there is no hope to get support from any quarter of the world; a fool devoid of any capability to plan for future is hopeless and for a man without any resource of any kind, the whole existence is barren of any hope.]

वरं वनं व्याघ्रगजेन्द्रसेवितं
द्रुमालयं पक्वपफलाम्बुसेवनं।
तृणेषु शया शतजीर्णवल्कलं
न बुन्धुमध्ये धनहीन जीवनम् ।। 152 ।।

Varam Vanam Vyaaghragajendra Sevitam
Drumaalayam Pakkvaphalaambusevanam.
Trineshu Shayaa Shatjeernavallkalam
Na Bandhumaddhye Dhanheena Jeevanam.

It is imprudent to stay in a jungle teeming with panthers and elephants; to dwell beneath the trees and survive by eating wild fruits and drinking (unchecked) water; to sleep on the bed made of wild straw and wear clothes made of the bark of the trees. But, if one is forced to dwell among his close relations as a pauper it is better to go and stay in the jungles under the conditions explained above rather than stay there.

[Meaning that if a person is poor and moneyless; he had better stay in a jungle suffering the most wild conditions rather than stay as a pauper among his relations.]

अनागत विधता च प्रत्युत्पन्नमतिस्तथा।
द्वावेतौ सुखमेवेते यद्धविश्यो विनश्यति ।। 153 ।।

Anaagat vidhaataa Cha Prattutpannamatistathaa.
Dvaavetau Sukhameveta Yaddbhavishyo Vinashyati.

He who is aware of the future troubles and possesses sharp intelligence remains happy. In contradistinction to this stage, he who remains inactive, waiting for the good days to come destroys his own life.

[A far-sighted and intelligent person is able to tackle the troubles far more efficiently than that fatalist sluggard who eventually gets destroyed by his lack of foresight and inactivity.]

मूर्खस्तु परिहर्तव्य: प्रत्यक्षो द्विपद: पशु:।
भिनत्ति वाक्यशूलेन अदृश्ययं कण्टकं यथा ।। 154 ।।

Moorkhastu Paribartavyah Prattyaksho Dvipadah Pashuh.
Bhinattih Vaakyashoolen Adrishyayam Kantakam Yathaa.

One should cease contact with the fools, regarding them as the biped animals, because they sting us by their senseless speech as though they are piercing an invisible thorn.

[A man devoid of common intelligence is like a two-footed animal. He stings us by his speech. Though we can't see the thorn, we feel its pinch caused by his incisive words.]

मांसमक्ष्यै: सुरापानैमखैश्छांस्रवर्जितै:।
पशुभि: पुरुषाकैरण्क्रांताऽस्ति च मेदिनी ।। 155 ।।

Maansmakshayaih Suraapaanaimarkhaishchaastravarjitaih.
Pashubih Purishaakaarainkraantaasti Cha Medinee.

A meat-eater, a wine-taker and a fool are animals in the human form. The earth is getting distressed by their weight.

[Chanakya regards meat-eaters, (liquor) wine-takers and fools as animals, despite their human form. All the three category-people, do not apply their intelligence to discern what is good for them and what is harmful. It is only the power of discretion to distinguish between good and evil that makes a man out of his beastly inclinations. Hence the observation.]

हस्तौ दानवर्जितौ श्रुतिपुटौ सारस्वतद्रोहिणौ
नेत्रो साधुविलोकरहिते पादौ न तीर्थं गतौ।
अन्यायार्जितदित्तपूर्णमुदरं गर्वेणं तुंगं शिरौ
रे रे जम्बुक मुञ्च-मुञ्च सदसा नीचं सुनिन्द्यं वपुः ।। 156 ।।

Hastau Daanvarjitau Shrutimputau Saaraswatdrohinau
Netre Saadhuvilokrahite Paadau Na Teerth Gatau.
Anny aayaarjitadittapoornanudaram Garvenam Tungam Shirau
Re Re Jambuck Munch-Munch Sadasaa Neecham Suninddyam Vapuh.

The hands didn't give any alms, the ears didn't hear any knowledgeable discourse, the eyes didn't have any Darshan of a Sadhu, the feet didn't go to any sacred place, the belly is filled with food earned through unlawful and immoral means–yet still you hold your head arrogantly high ! O Jackal! Quit your this (useless) body forthwith !!

[Chanakya says that deem that arrogant person to be not a man but jackal who gives no alms, hears no knowledgeable discourse, sees no Sadhu, goes to sacred place and fills his belly with food earned through immoral means. Such a man is verily a jackal and must quit his body immediately.]

विप्रास्मिन्नगरे महान् कथय कस्ताल द्रुमाणां गण:
को दाता रजको ददाति वसनं प्रातगृर्हीत्वा निशि।
को दक्ष: पवित्तदारहरण सर्वेऽपि दक्षा: जना:
कस्माज्जीवति हे सखे विषकृमिन्यायेन जीवास्यहम् ।। 157 ।

Vippraasminnagre Mahan Kathaya Kasttal Drumaanaam Ganah
Ko Datta Rajako Dadaati Vasanam Praatgrihittvaa Nishi.
Ko Dakshah Parivittadadraharana Sarveapi Dakshaah Janaah
Kasmajeevati He Sakhe Vishkriminyaayen Jeevaassyaham.

"O friend! Who is big (great) in this town? The Palm trees? Who is the most charitable person? The washer-man who takes (dirty) clothes and brings back (after washing) in the evening? Who is the shrewd and intelligent here? He who steals others' wealth and others' woman. Then how do you survive in this town?" "Just like an insect in the gutter:"

[Chanakya says in this dramatic style that the town where no wise, intelligent, noble or scholarly person dwell, where people may not be deft and efficient but expert in looting others and each vying with others in bad manners and roguery, should be considered just a pile of filth or a gutter and whose citizens just the herd of insects.]

आहरनिद्रा भय मैथुनानि
समानि चैतानि नृणा पशूनाम्।
ज्ञानो नराणामधिी विशेषा
ज्ञानेन हीना पशुभि: समाना।। 158 ।।

Aahaarninddraa Bhaya Maithanaani
Samaani Chaitaani Nrinaam Pashunaam.
Gyaano Naraanaamadhiko Vishesho
Gyaanen Heena Pashubhih Samaanaah.

All beings, including human beings need food, sleep, sex as their natural requirement and all experience the common emotion of fear (of the unknown). But discretionary power alone rests with the humans. Hence the man who is devoid of discretion is just an animal.

(Eating food when hungry, sleeping when exhausted, indulging in sexual intercourse and fearings. Discretion endows man with the capacity to distinguish between the good and the evil, between knowledge and ignorance, etc. Obviously the person who is lacking in discretion or who has no discretionary powers is verily a beast.)

येषां न विद्या न तपो, न दानव
न चापि शीलं न गुणो न धर्मः।
ते मर्त्यलोके भूवि भारभूता
मनुष्यरूपेड मृगाश्चरन्ति ।।159।।

Yeshaam Na Viddya no Tapo Na Daanam
Na Chaapi Sheelam Na Guno Na Dharamah.
Te Mrittuloke Bhuvi Bhaarbhootaa
Manushyaroopen Mrigaashcharanti.

Those who have no education or knowledge, no determination, no charitable disposition, no manners, no virtuous qualities and no firm faith are just a dead load on this earth. They ate verily beasts in human form roaming about on the earth.

[i.e., a man should be educated with the capacity to undergo penance to achieve certain objectives; he ought to have a charitable disposition, good manners, virtuous qualities and firm faith in his religion or belief. If a man lacks these, he is just a biped animal.]

धर्मार्थकाममोक्षेषु यस्यैकोऽपि न विद्यते।
जन्म जन्मानि मर्त्येषु मरणं तस्य केवलम् ।। 160।।

Dharmaarthakaamamokshesbu Yassyai Koapi Na Viddyate.
Jannma Jannmaani Mattyaryeshu Maranam Tassya Kevalam.

That man who fails to achieve even one of the four aims of life, viz. Dharma (faith in his belief), Artha (riches which provide meaning to life), Kaam (Fulfilment of the desires), and Moksha (satiation of all wants) is verily born only for dying (as his life is just a waste).

मुहूर्तमपि जीवेच्च नरः शुक्लेन कर्मणा।
न कल्पमपि कष्टेन लोक द्वय विरोधिना ।। 161।।

Muhoortamapi Jeevecha Naraha Shukklen Karmanaa.
Na Kalpamapi Kashten Lok Dvaya Virodhinaa.

A momentary existence involved in a highly noble work is any time better than survival for ages but working against the welfare of this world and the next. [A man doing some noble deeds and living for a very short duration is more welcome in this world than a man living for centuries but working against the welfare of all.]

येषां श्रीमद्यशोदासुत पदकमले नास्ति भक्तिर्नराणां
येषां माभीरकन्याप्रियगुणकथने नानुक्ता च जिह्वा।
येषां श्रीकृष्णलीलाललितरसकथा सादरौ नव कर्णौ
धिक्तां-धिक्तां धिकेतान् कथयति सततं कीर्तनस्थोमृदंगः ।।162।।

Yeshaam Shreemaddyashodaasut Padakamale Naasti Bhaktirnaraanaa
Yeshaam Maabheerkannyaapriyagunakathane Naanuraktaa Cha Jivhaa.
Yeshaam Shree Krishnaleelaalalitrashkathaa Saadarau Nava Karnau
Dhiktaam-Dhitaam Dhiketaan Kathyayati Satatam Keeertanshthomridangah

He who has no devotion for the lotus feet of the son of mother Yashoda (Krishna); who doesn't chant the noble attributes of the daughter of Aahirs (Radha); whose ears do not get tuned to hearing the juicy description of the sportive play of Lord Krishna receive the censure form the 'Mridang-bols' saying "Dhikta-Dhikta, Dhiketan" (meaning fie upon him! fie upon him! fie upon him!!!' [Chanakya says that he who has no love or devotion for Lord Krishna, the son of mother Yashoda; and for Radha, the daughter of Aahirs (Radha) is wasting his life in the world. Deftly using the bols' (the rhythmic sounds) of Mridang to convey his abhorence for such person, he conveys his meaning very onomatopoetically that "fie upon such man!"

धर्मार्थकाममोक्षाणां यस्यैकोऽपि न विद्यते।
अजागलस्तनस्येव तस्य जन्म निरर्थकम् ।।163।।

Dharmaarthakaamamokhaanaam Yessyaikoapi Na Viddyate.
Ajaagalastanasyeva Tassya Jannma Nirathakam.

He who fails to achieve even one of the four aims of life:

Dharm, Artha, Kaam and Moksha has his life as useless as breast below the neck of the goat (which has no purpose, and is just useless).

स जीवति गुणा यस्य यस्य धर्म स जीवति।
गुण धर्म विहिनस्य जीवितं निष्प्रयोजनम् ।। 164।।

Sa Jeevati Gunaa Yasya Yasya Dharama sa jeevati.
Guna Dharma vihinasya Jeevitam Nishprayjanam.

Only he survives who is virtuous; only he lives who is firm in his Dharma. He who is devoid of virtues and faith (Dharma) is existing in vain.

[Virtues and firmness in faith make life meaningful. Those who lack these qualities are wasting their life.]

न यातं पदमीश्वरस्य विध्वित्संसारविच्छत्तये
स्वर्गद्वारकपाटपाटनपटु धर्मोपि नोपार्जितः।
नारीपीनपयोध्रयुगलं स्वप्नेपि नालिंगितं
मातुःकेवलमेव यौवनच्छेदकुठारो वयम् ।। 165।।

Na Dhyaatam Paadmeeshvarassya vidhivattsamsaarvichattye
Svargadvaarakapaat Paatanpatuh Dharmoapi Nopaarjitaah.
Naareepeenpayodharyugalam Svappneapi Naalingitam
Maatuh Kevalmeva Yauvanchedkutharo Vayam.

Neither we devoted our concentration of the feet of Lord Almighty to get release from the mundane bonds, nor we accrued religious merit to ensure our niche in the heaven, nor even in dreams we ever passionately embraced the solid softness of a woman's breasts. Thus, except of acting as an axe on our mother's youthful beauty, what else did we achieve in the world?

[Chanakya explains in this quatrain symbolically the attainments of the three basic alms: Moksha, Dharma and Kaam, whose achievement automatically ensures Artha, the last of the attributes. Release from the mundane world means Moksha; accrual of the religious merit ensures the adherence to Dharma and the excitement to embrace the hard breasts of a woman symbolically represents Kaam: In short, the meaning of this quatrain is that one wastes one's life without attaining fulfilment of any of the four attributes explained above. Also, the fact is that delievery of a child entails decay of the youth on the part of the mother. So, if one has not attained fulfilment in any of the four attributes, what else the purpose of one's birth be except ruining one's mother's beauty.]

Who is More Cunning?

नारायणां नापितो धूर्तः पक्षिणां चैव वायसः।
चतुष्पदां श्रृगालस्तु स्त्रीणां धूर्ता च मालिनी ।। 166 ।।

Naraanaam Naapito Dhoortah Pakshinaam Chaiv Vaayashah.
Chatushpadaam Shrigaalasya Streenaam Dhoortaa Cha Maalinee.

Barber among men; the crow among birds; the jackal among the four legged beasts; and the female gradener among the women is cunning.

Vain Attempt

अन्यथा वेदपाण्डित्यं शास्त्रामाचारमन्यथा।
अन्यथा वदत: शान्तं लोका:क्लिश्यन्ति चान्यथा ।। 167 ।।

Annyathaa Vedapaandittyam Shaastramaachaarmannyatha.
Annyatha Vadatha Shaantam Lokaah Klishyanti Channyathaa.

Those who try to speak foul of the Vedas; the erudition, the scriptures, the noble conduct and the peace-loving man make a vain attempt.

The Wicked: the Snake

दुर्जनेषु च सर्पेषु वरं सर्पो न दुर्जन:।
सर्पो दशति कालेन दुर्जनस्तु पदे-पदे। ।। 168 ।।

Durjaneshu Cha Sarpeshu Varam Sarpo Na Durjanah.
Sarpo Dashaati Kaalen Durjanastu Pade-pade.

Between the wicked and the snake, the snake is less evil because it stings once while the wicked stings on every step. [Snake would sting rarely and once but the wicked would sting repeatedly and even most unobstrusively. Hence the wicked is more dangerous than even a snake.]

Most poisonous

तक्षकस्य विषं दन्ते मक्षिकाया मुखे विशम्।
वृश्चिकस्य विषं पुच्दे सवागे दुर्जने विषम् ।। 169 ।।

Takshasya Visham Dante Makshikaayaa Mukhe Visham.
Vrishchikasya Visham Puche Sarvaange Durjane Visham.

The place of poison in a snake is the tooth, in a fly the head, in a scorpion the tail but the wicked has poison in his entire body. [Meaning that a wicked person is much more deadly than all the poisonous insects and reptiles put together. Hence we must guard against the wicked.]

The Hellish Souls

अत्यन्तलेप: च वाणी
दरिद्रता च स्वजनेषु वैरम्।
नीच प्रसंग: कुलहीनसेवा
चिह्नानि देहे नरकस्थितानाम् ।। 170 ।।

Attyantlepah Katutaa Cha Vaanee
Daridrataa Cha Svajaneshu Vairam.
Neech Prasangah Kuleensevaa
Chinnhaani Dehe Narkasthikaanaam.

Fiery temper, bitter speech, poverty, rancour for one's own relations, slavery of the lowly persons and association with the rogues – these are some of the sure signs of a hellis soul. [A wicked person is invariably very short tempered with bitter speech and rancour and jealousy for his own kith and kin. Moreover, he has very bad relations with his own people. He would gladly serve the low persons and would move in the company of the rogues. Such a man should be deemed to be an incarnation of some evil spirit.]

Other's Happiness

तुष्यन्ति भोजने विप्रा मयूरा घनगर्जिते।
साधवः परसम्पत्तौ खला:पर विपत्तितषु:।। 171 ।।

Tushyanti Bhojane Vipraa Mayooraa Ghanagarjite.
Saadhavah Porasampattauh Khalah Par Vipattishuh.

The brahmans become pleased with food, the peacocks by hearing the thunder of the clouds, the noble by seeing other's prosprity and the wicked by witnessing other's distress.

The Wicked Nature

न दुर्जनः साधुदशामुपैति
बहुत प्रकारैरऽपि शिक्ष्यमाणः।
आमूलसिक्तं पयसा धृतेन
न निम्बवृक्षेः मधुरत्वमेति ।। 172 ।।

Na Durjanah Saadhudashaamupaiti
Bhautprakaarairapi Shikshyamaanah.
Aamoolasiktam Payassa Ghriten
Na Nimbavrikshoh Madhurattvameti.

No method can trun a wicked into a noble person like as no quantity of milk and ghee can turn the neem tree sweet. [The basic nature can't be altered.]

दुर्जनं सज्जनं कर्तुमुपायो न हि भूतले।
अपनं शतघाघौतान श्रेष्ठमिन्द्रियं भवेत् ।। 173 ।।

Durjanam Sajjanam Kartumupaayo Nahi Bhootale.
Apaanam Shatghaaghautaanna Shreshthamindriyam Bhavet.

There is no way on the earth by which a bad man be made a good man. Even if one washes the anus region a hundred times, it can't be made a pious organ, [Chankya asserts by this sweeping statement that the evil can't be made good no matter what means one adopts to achieve this aim. It is as good as trying to wash the anus region to turn it into a pious opening, which it can never be.]

वयसः परिणामे हि यः खलः खल एव सः ।
सुपक्कमपि माधुर्य नोपायतीन्द्रवारुणम् ।। 174 ।।

Vayasah Parinaame Hiyahkhalah Khalah Evasah.
Supakkvamapi Madhurya Nopaayateendravaarunam.

Even till the fag end of his life the wicked continues to be wicked. The indravarun fruit (a very bitter fruit) cannot become sweet even when it is well-ripe. [Wickedness of one's character has no effect of age. The wicked person will remain wicked even if he turns old like the bitter fruit of Indravarun, which doesn't become sweet even when it is fully ripe.]

दह्यमानां सुतीव्रेण नीचाः परयशोग्निना।
अशक्तास्तत्पदं गन्तुं ततो निन्दा प्रकुर्वते ।। 175 ।।

Dahyamaanaam Suteevrena Neechaah Paryashoagninaa.
Ashaktaast attpadam Gautum Tato Nindaam Prakurvate.

The wicked burns with the fire of jealousy seeing the prosperity of others. Since he cannot progress (due to his shortcomings), he starts deriding others.

[He who is jealous at other's prosperity is basically an incompetent person. Knowing his shortcomings he realises that he can't achieve what others have done. But, his wicked nature refuses to admit anyone's superiority. So he starts finding faults and deriding others to mentally efface the element of their superiority, only to assert his parity. It is a known psychological truth which Chanakya had opined milleniums ago, but it is still very true.]

हस्ती हस्तसहस्रेण शहतहुस्रे वाजिन:।   श्रृगिरी दशहस्तेन देशत्यागेन दुर्जन: ।। 176 ।।

Hastee Hastasahastren Shathasten Vaajinah.
Shringinee Dashahasten Deshttyaagen Durjanah.

Keep the distance of one thousand hands between an elephant and yourself, one hundred hands between a horse and yourself, ten hands between the animals with horn and yourself and a full country between the wicked and yourself

[Chanakya has used the measure of the hand's length only to make objective a subjective assertion. In short, he tries to bring home his point that the wicked is far more dangerous than all the basts. Keeping "full country between yourself and the wicked" means that one shouldn't stay in the land inhabited by the wicked.]

खलानां कण्टकानां च द्विविधैव प्रतिक्रिया।   उपनामुखभंगों वा दूरतैव विसर्जनम् ।। 177 ।।

Khalaanaam Kantakaanaam Cha Dvividhaiv Pratikriyaa.
Upaanaamukhbango Vaadoorataive Visarjanam.

There are only two ways the wicked and the thorns should be dealt with: crush them by your shoes or go away from them.

[Meaning either smash them to bits or have no contact with them. They shouldn't be dealt with leniently.]

हस्ती त्वंकुशमात्रोण बाजी हस्तेन तापते।
श्रंगालकुटहस्तेन खड्गहस्तेन दुर्जन: ।। 178 ।।

Hastee Tvamkushmaatrena Baajee Hasten Taapate.
Shringaalkhuhasten Khadaghasten Durjanah.

An elephant is kept under control by a goad, the horse by hand, the animals with horns by hand or stick and the wicked by a sword (or any Such weapon).

[The emphasis is again on being ruthless in our dealing with the wicked.]

कृते प्रतिकृतिं कुर्यात् हिंसेन प्रतिहिंसनम्।
तत्रा दोषो न पतति दुष्टे दौष्ट्यं समाचरेत् ।। 179 ।।

Krite Pratikritim Kurryaat Hinsen Pratihinsanam.
Putra Dosho na Patati Dushte Daushttyam Samaacharet.

Meet obligation with obligation, voilence with vengeance and wicked with wickedness. There is no harm in acting foully with the foul persons.

सत्कुले योजनयेत्कन्या पुत्रां विद्यासु योजयेत्।
व्यसने योजयेच्छत्रुं मित्रं धर्मे नियोजयेत् ।। 180 ।।

Sattkule Yojayettkannyaaa Putram Viddyaasu Yojayet.

Vyasane Youjayechatrum Mitram Dharme Niyojet.

Marry your daughter into a noble family, employ your son into studies, engage your friend in good deeds and involve your enemy in the evil practices.

[Marrying the daughter off into a good family; providing best possible education to the son; engaging the friend in good deeds and hoodwinking your enemy to involve him in some evil practices constitute a 'must' job in Chanakya's view. He is one of those few thinkers who didn't mince words when he exhorted all to adopt evil means to overcome an evil if need be. There is nothing immoral, for example, if we take recourse to speaking lies to subdue a liar.]

क: काल: कानि मित्राणि को देश: को व्ययागमो: ।
कस्याहं का च मे शक्तिरित चिन्तयं मुहुर्मुहु: ।। 181।।

Kah Kaalah Kaani Mitraani Kodeshah ko Vyayaagamoh.
Kasyaaham Kaa Chame Shaktirit Chinttyam Muhurmuhuh.

How are the times? Who is a friend? What type of land is this? What is the income and what is the expenditure? What am I and how much power I really possess?–all these questions one must keep asking oneself.

[Before entering into any venture, we must assess our position minutely. Most of the failures are caused by assessing only our strengths and not our weaknesses. We must weigh the pros and cons fully before doing anything. Only then can we expect successful results.]

दाक्षिण्यं स्वजने दया परजने शाठ्यं सदा दुर्जने
प्रीतिः साधुजने स्मय खलजने विद्वज्जने चार्जवम्।
शौर्य शत्रुजने क्षमागुरुजने नारीजने धूर्तताः।
इत्थं ये पुरुषा कलासु कुशलास्तेष्वेव लोकस्थितिः ।। 182 ।।

Daakshinnyam Svajane Dayaa Parjane Shaathyam Sadaa Durjane
Preetih Saadhujane Smayay Khalijane Viddvajjane Charjjvam.
Shaurya Shatrujane Kshamaa Gurujane Naareenjane Dhoortataah
Ittham Ye Purushaa Kalaasu Kushalaasteshvev lokasthitiha.

They who treat their own people with love; others with kindness; who are ruthless to the wicked; straight forward to the noble; indifferent to the fool; respectful to the scholars; who take on their enemey with bravery and pay obeisance to the Gurus; who are not infatuated to the woman–they are known as great men.

[In this quatrain, Chanakya has very succinctly sums up the ideal behaviour of a man with his society. Quid pro quo is the basic idea behind this behaviour.]

Allegiance

यत्रोदकस्तत्रा वसन्ति हंसा
स्तथैव शुष्कं परित्यजन्ति।
न हंसतुल्येन नरेण भाव्यं
पुनस्तयजन्तः पुनराश्रयन्तः ।। 183 ।।

Yatrodakastatra Vasanti Hansaa
Stathaiv Shuskam Parittyajanti.

Na Hansatullyen Naren Bhaavyam
Punastayaajantah Punaraashrayantah.

The swans dwell in the pond full of water. The moment its water dries they desert it. But man shouldn't be like them to relinquish a place and again return to it.

[Through this quatrain Chanakya expresses his opinion on allegiance. He says that the swans are basically the opportunistic and selfish. They stay for their own comfort and leave the pond heartlessly, without thinking about the agony the poor pond might be suffering. A man should not be so selfish but should live with his benefactor through weal and woe.]

Foremost Duty

धर्म धनं च धन्यं च गुरोर्वचनमौषध्म्।
संगृहीतं च कर्तव्यमन्यथा न तु जीवति ।। 184 ।।

Dharma Dhanam Cha Dhaannyamcha Gurorvachanmaushadham
Sangraheetam Cha Kartavyamannyathaa Natu Jeevati.

One must go on accumulating religious merit, money, eatables, the teachings of the Guru and (herbal) medicines or else one can't survive.

[Here eatables means all those edible things, which could be preserved. Medicines means all the herbal medicines roots, etc. During the period of Chanakya, these herbs were the only source to procure, or prepare medicines from. The more one had them, the more his chances of recovery from any illness. Rest of the 'must' things are self evident.]

त्यज दुर्जनसंसर्ग भज साधुसमागमम्।
कुरु पुण्यमहोरात्रं स्मर नित्यमनित्यत: ।। 185 ।।

Tyaj Durjan Sansarga Bhaj Saadhu Sammagamam.
Kuru Punnyamahoraatram Smar Nittyamanittyatah.

One must shun the company of the wicked and seek association of the noble; one must keep on doing good deeds without foregetting Lord Almighty even for a moment.

अनन्तशास्त्रां बहुलाश्च विद्या
अल्पं द कालो बहुविघ्नता च।
आसानभूतं तदुपासनीयं
हसो यथा क्षीरमिवाम्बुपयात् ।। 186 ।।

Anantashaastram Bahilaashcha Viddyaa
Alpam Dakaalo Bhauvighnataa Cha.
Aasabhootam Tadupaasneeyam
Hanso Yathaa Ksheermivaambupaddhyaat.

There are infinite scriptures, unlimited branches of knowledge but human life is very short with many hurdles in that short duration. Hence one should, like the swan who makes clear distinction between milk and water even if they be mixed and drinks pure milk, drive the useful essence of all learning and discard the rubbish.

[Meaning that the sea of knowledge is very vast and life is short–so one should suck out the essence of all learning and cast aside the useless information by clearly sifting them through one's discertion.]

तद् भोजनं यद् द्विज भुक्तशेषं
तत्सौहृदं यत्क्रियते परस्मिन्।
सा प्रज्ञता या न करोति पाप
दम्भं विना यः क्रियते स धर्मः ।। 187 ।।

Tadḍ Bhojanam Yadd Dvij Bhuktashesham
Tattsauhridam Yattkriyate Parasmin.
Saa Praagyataa Yaana Karoti Paap
Dambham Vinaa Yaha Kriyate Sadharmah.

Food is that which is left over by the brahmans after having it to their bellyful; love is consideration for others; wisdom is that which prevents one from committing sin and noble religious act (Dharma) is that doing which one doesn't feel arrogance.

[i.e. One must eat after feeding the brahmans. We all love our own kith and kin but real love is that when we feel for others. Wisdom is that which saves one from committing sin. And we must not have the feeling of arrogance when indulging in the acts of charity, for if one does any good thing for others with the sense of the 'doership' one loses all merit, according to the ancient Indian thought. Chanakya has merely repeated the same thought.]

गतं शोको न कर्तव्य भविष्यं नैव चिन्तयेत्।
वर्तमानेन कालेन प्रवर्तन्ते विचक्षणाः ।। 188 ।।

Gatam Shoko Na Kartavya Bhavishyam Naiv Chintayet.
Vartamaanen Kaalen Pravartante Vishakshanaah.

One should not grieve for the past and worry for the

future. The wise care for the present and chart their life's course accordingly.

[Care for the present sets right not only the past but also the future. The wise don't cry on the split milk nor worry for the future.]

परोपकरणं येषां जागर्ति हृदये सताम्।
नश्यन्ति विपदस्तेषां सम्पदः स्यु पदे-पदे ।। 189 ।।

Paropkarnam Yeshaan Jaagaarti Hridaye Sataam.
Nashyanti Vipadasteshaam Sampadah Syu Pade-Pade.

Those who have consideration for others have their problems getting solved or destroyed automatically and they receive (unseen) benefits at every step.

[Those who act good for others receive their goodness in reciprocation, solving their own problems. Yudhisthar says that if you aim at other's benefit, your own selfish end would also be served in the process.]

यस्माच्च प्रियमिच्छेत् तस्य ब्रू यात्सदा प्रियम्।
व्याधे मृगवधं गन्तु गीतं गायति सुस्वरम् ।। 190 ।।

Yasmaacha Priyamichhet Tassya Broo Yaatsadaa Priyam.
Vyaagho Mrigvadham Gantu Geetam Gaayati Suswaram.

Speak sweet before someone you expect a favour from. When the fowler spots a deer he sings a mellifluous song before killing it.

[This Shloka is full of practical modern sense also, for people have grown quite shrewd-perhaps by following this dictum! The fowler and hunter must cover up their intention so as not to appear blantantly selfish. Preparation of the ground, which must be conducive for the germination of the seed is a compulsory 'fore-act' before sowing the seed!]

अत्यासन्न विनाशाय द्रूरस्था न पफलप्रदा।
सेव्यतां मयभागेन राजवगिुरुस्त्रिाय: ।। 191 ।।

Attyaasann Vinaashaaya Doorasthaa Na Phalapradaa.
Sevyataam Maddhyabhaagen Rajvahinagurnestriyah.

Staying close to the king, fire, the Guru and woman yield disastrous result, but staying far away from them do not produce any good result either. So, we must chose the mean position, i.e. we shouldn't be very far off from or very near to them.

[Proximity with the king might give some occasional benefit but the situation would expose one to the royal wrath consequence might be disastrous. The same is true with fire, woman and the Guru.]

एक एव पदार्थस्तु त्रिधा भवति वीक्षति।
कुपणं कामिनी मासं योगिभि: कामिभि: श्वभि ।। 192 ।।

Ekeva Padaarthastu Tridhaa Bhavati Veekshaati.
Kupanam Kaamineem Maansam Yogibhih Shvabhi.

The same object–the body of a woman–may be viewed differently by three different persons. The lecher sees it as the source of sexual gratification, the Yogi as a filthy, foul smelling corpse and the dogs as luscious meat.

[Chanakya says that the viewed object creates different impressions in different observers according to their basic nature. It all depends on how one looks at it. The lecher, ever intent upon having his sexual lust gratified looks at a woman's body, through dead with sexually starved eyes. The Yogi, ever searching for dead would look at it as an object helping him in consummating his worship and a dog, ever-hungry for meat, looks at it as a luscious food. Chanakya subtly hints that the value of the viewed object, like beauty lies in the eyes of the beholder.]

मणिर्लुण्ठति पादाग्रे काचः शिरसि धार्यते।
क्रय-विक्रयवेलायां काचः काचो मणिर्मणिः ।। 193 ।।

Manirlunthati Paadaagre Kaachah Shiriasi Dhaaryate
Kraya-Vikrayavelaayaam Kaachah Kaacho Manirnanih.

Notwithstanding the gems rolling at one's feet and the mere glass-objects kept on the head (respectfully), when the hour of bargaining for them for the sale arrives, the glass would be considered just the glass and the gems the priceless object.

[Chanakya says that the adverse circumstances might belittle one's position but they can't diminish one's intrinsic worth. When the time of reckoning arrives the glass-piece; however well kept won't match with the gem. The external conditions only marginally affect the intrinsic worth of any object. Dust might cover the gem to render it lustreless but sooner or later it must fetch its intrinsic value. Reality can't be hoodwinked by any trick for long.]

लोभश्चेदगुणेन किं पिशुनता यद्यस्ति किं पातकै:
सत्यं यत्तपसा च किं शुचिमनो यद्यस्ति तीर्थेन किम्।
सौजन्यं यदि किं गुणै सुमहिमा यद्यस्ति किं मडनै:
सद्विद्या यदि किं धनैरपयशो यद्यस्ति कि मृत्युना ।। 194 ।।

Lobhashchedagunen Kim Pishunataa Yaddyasti Ki Paatakaih
Sattyam Yattpasaa Chakim Shuchimano Yaddyasti Teerthen Kim.
Sanjannyam Yadi Kim Gunaih Sumahimaa Yaddyaasti Kim Mandanaih
Saddviddyaa Yadi Kim dhanairapayasho Yaddyaasti Kim Mrittyunaa.

Why must a greedy fellow be concerned with other's vices; a backbiter with sin; a truthful man with the performance of penance and austerities; a guileless heart with a visit to the sacred places; a celebrity with the want of self-decoration; a well educated man with wealth and an ill famed person with death? The greedy person hardly cares for other vices. If he can hope to usurp something from a most notorious person, he would not hesitate in doing so. Since greed is going to blind his vision, he looks at nothing else but at the desired object he covets for. The greedy would not be concerned whether the other one is a traitor or a patriot; what weighs most in his mind is the wealth that he possesses. He would be accepting anything from the most vile source if that satisfies his greed.

Similarly, the one finding fault with others is not concerned with his treading on the immoral or sinth path if it satisfies his urge. He would concoct stories, impute false motives to have his say. Back-biting tendency is a pathological ailment and the one who has this tendency won't be deterred even by the fear of committing a sin. And he, who is honest and truthful, doesn't need to indulge in self-torture, for all such selfinflictions are performed to purge all the vices from his mind. When he is already honest and truthful, it means he is clean and needs no such self-inflictions.

One goes to the sacred places apparently to earn merit which is the exclusive preserve of a guileless heart. Why must anyone go to wash his linen when it is already clean. The visits to the sacred places are supposed to make one guileless. When one is already guileless, why must one go to the sacred places? One wears good clothes, ornaments and does all sort of make ups only to be the cynosure of all eyes. But if one is already a celebrity, the need for such self-embellishments doesn't arise, for his celebrity status makes one automatically the cynosure of all eyes. His fame rivets all attention to his personality. In modern context, it can be said that why must Gandhiji be clad in three pieces suit to merit people's attention? Even if be clad in rags, it is he who would be the cynosure of all eyes and not a well-clad movie superstar?

The Indian thought avers that the real education is that which liberates: (☒☒ ☒☒☒☒ ☒☒ ☒☒☒☒☒☒) says the Upanishad. And wealth plus all mundane considerations bind one to these transient fallacies. Obviously, both are contradictory to each other. Good education liberates and wealth hinds. So, why should a well-educated or a liberated soul crave for wealth and other material possessions.

Lastly, an ill-reputed or ill-famed person leads an already condemned life. It is virtually death that he undergoes in the condemned state. Since he is already as good as dead, death brings in no change. So an ill-famed person is hardly concerned with death.

राजा वेश्या यमश्चाग्निः चौराः बालकयाचकाः।
परदुःखं न जानन्ति अष्टमोग्रामकण्टकः ।। 195 ।।

Raajaa Veshyaa Yamashchaagnih Chauraah Baalakyaachakaah.

Pardukham Najaananti Ashtamograamakantakah.

The king, the prostitute, the death-god Yamaraj, fire, thief, beggar, child and the persons (of the village) who enjoy making others fight. These eight kinds of persons do not experience the trouble of others. [If the king starts feeling the troubles of his subjects individually, he cannot run his state. For an efficient administration what the king should be concerned with is the overall problem of the subjects or of the society and not with the individual subject. If he does so, he can't implement any of his rules or laws because some of them are bound to trouble someone individually. The prostitute is obviously unconcerned with her customer's problems. Her only concern is to extrot as much money from him against the services she provides him avail at her brothel. She has to be impervious to her client's personal problems to succeed in her profession.

[Similarly] death-god, Yamaraj cannot be individually concerned with anyone's problem. This is a mechanical system, wherein, the person should die the moment his age expires. Like Yamaraj fire is also impersonal all, whether a live or dead. A beggar is always so overawed by his problems of survival that he has no time to think for others. The thief has to be impersonal or else he would fail miserably. And the child is hardly conscious of the other's problem due to his limited understanding. The most damaging among the lot is that disturbing person who loves to make people fight with each other. He derives saddistic pleasure out of such fights. If he also starts appreciating other's problems he just can go ahead whatever he relishes most.]

सुसिद्धमौषधं धर्म गृहछिद्रं च मैथुनम्।
कुभुक्तं कुश्रुतं चैव मतिमान्न प्रकाशयेत् ।। 196 ।।

Sushiddhamaushadham Dharm Grihachiddram Chamaithunaṃ

Kubhuktam Kushrutam Chaiv Matimaann Prakashyet.

The wise man must always keep his secret concerning the following informations: about the efficacious medicines, about his Dharma (faith), the short comings of his household, his sexual contact, the rotten food already consumed and the bad or evil things heard by them. [It is a age old belief that if one finds a particular medicine quite effective, I would lose its efficacy if told about it openly. One should never declared, about his duty or faith or make a propaganda of it. The essence of a faith or a religious duty lies in its faithful adherence and not in its publicity. For, in that case you open yourself to criticism from others which might result in your becoming sceptical about it. Chanakya's this assertion indirect contradiction to the prevalent practice of the modren times. Now the people believe more in the publicity of their faith. No 'Jagaran' or 'puja' is deemed complete unless accompanied by blaring you speakers and droning chants of the Mantras. This militant adherence a one's faith and the accompanying show of it provoke others and cause disharmony in the society. In this context, Chanakya's this observation appears full of relevant veracity.] It is pure common sense to hide you or your household shortcomings. Their exposure would bring you much less accolades for your simplicity but too many damaging remarks. Similarly, only a fool would spill out the details of one's sexual contacts, even with one's legally wedded wife. These things are not to be told but cherished and enjoyed in privacy.

If the rotten food is already consumed there is no sense in Advertising about it. Suppose one has taken the soup with a dead fly in it. Chances are that it might not cause any ill – effect but if one is told about it, then psychologically it might create some disturbance in the system of the listener. Moreover, if one has eaten anything which is prohibited by one's religion or society, there is no sense in advertising about it.

The last observation is very meaningful. Often we hear something wrong about some person or some event. It is prudent not to give currency to it by telling others about it, for this is how a rumour spreads. Moreover, if in the fit of rage one mouth palpably something wrong about some one, your passing it to others' may cause unwanted controversy. It is better not only from the personal but social point of view also. Do digest it rather than disseminate it.

तृणं लघु तृणात्तूलं तूलादपि च चाचकः।
वायुना किं न जीतोऽसौ मामायं याचयिष्यति ।। 197 ।।

Trinam Laghu Trinaattoolam Toolaadapi Cha Yaachakah
Vaayunaa Kirmna Jeetoasau Maamyam Yaachyishyati.

A straw is very light but cotton is even lighter than it and a suppliant (or a beggar) is lighter than even cotton. Then why doesn't the wind fly it away? It is because the wind is apprehensive lest it should start going something from it also.

[It is an oblique way of saying that begging is the meanest work. The satire and the punch of the saying are apparent.]

उत्यां कोऽपि महीधरो लधुतरो दोर्म्यां धृती लीलया
तेन त्वं दिवि भूतले च सततं गोवर्धनो गीयसे।
त्वां त्रैलोक्यधरं वहायि कुचयोरप्रेण नो गण्यते
किं वा केशव भाषणेन बहुना पुण्यं यशसा लभ्यते ।। 198 ।।

Uttyaam Koapi Maheedharo Laghutaro Dommaryaam Dhritee Leelayaa
Ten Tvam Divi Bhootale Cha Statam Govardhano Geeyase.
Tvaam Trai Lokkyatharam Vahaayi Kuchayorgrena No Gannyate
Kim Vaakeshav Bhaashanen Bahunaa Punuyam Yashasaa Labhyate.

Only because you could lift a small hill known as Goverdhan by your hand, you are in the heaven and the earth. And while you support all the three realms yet I hold you on the point of my breasts but I come in no reckoning. No need of saying more, O Krishna! tell me does one come in fame by dint of one's (past earned) merit? [Making a complaint to Lord Krishna in a poetic way, the Gopi says that the Lord is known as Goverdhan (lifter) (he who lifted the hill called Goverdhan) in the heaven and the earth only because the Lord could do so by his hand. While she holds the Lord, the supporter of the three realms (the heaven, the earth and the Patal lok or Nether world), on the tip of her breasts in the most affectionate and intimate way, yet no one praises here for her about this marveollous feat.

Then she asks Lord Krishna whether one earns merit not by one's present doing but by one's already existing celebrity status? Chanakya says in this poetic manner that those in fame have their tiny achievements magnified but a common man's great achievements are not even taken notice of this comparitive allegory used by Chanakya in expressing this pithy observation goes to prove the lingual command and the poetic conjecture of this great man otherwise renowned for his scheming manipulations.

General Observations

मूर्खशिष्योपदेशेन दुष्टास्त्रीभरणेन चं।
दु:खिर्त: सम्प्रयोगेण पण्डितोऽप्यवसीदति ।। 199 ।।

Moorkhashishyopadeshen dushtastreebharanen Cha.
Dukhitaih Samprayogen Panditoappyavaseedati.

Even the wise suffer grief by preaching a dunce pupil, supporting a vile woman and associating themselves with the melancholic persons:

[Instructing a dunce is a futile effort, for he has no capacity to assimilate whatever he is taught. Supporting a vile woman means creating a danger for the entire society: Association with the melancholic people is infectious as it would cause sadness in the person who even tries to console them. Of course, one may sympathise with them but association with them is imprudent.]

दुष्टा भार्या शठं मित्रां भृत्यश्चोत्तरदायक:।
ससर्पे गृहे वासो मृत्युरेव न संशय: ।। 200 ।।

Dushtaa Bhaarya Shatham Mitram Bhrittyshchottaradaayakah.
Sasarpe Grihe Vaaso Mrittyureva Na Sanshayah.

Wicked wife, roguish friend, impudent servant and stay in a sanke infested house cause death. There is no doubt about it.

[Since all the condidtion are self evident, they do not need seperate explanations.]

न निर्मिता केन न दृष्टपूर्वा न श्रूयते हेममयी कुरंगी।
तथाऽपि तृष्णा रघुनंदनस्य विनाशकाले विपरीतबुद्धिः ॥ 201 ॥

Na nirmitaa Ken Na drishtpoorvaa Na Shrooyate Hemamayi Kurangee.
Tathaapi Trishnaa Raghunandanassya Vinaashakaale Vipreetabuddhih.

No one did ever see or hear about any golden doe nor it was ever created, still behold the craving of Raghunandan! Indeed one's wisdom fails at the onset of the evil days.

[Chanakya expresses wonder that how Lord Ram could lie lured by that golden doe – for which Sita forced him to go and get it for herself, when no such doe was ever created, seen or heard about by anyone. Regrettably, he says that indeed the onset of evil days is heralded by the failure of one's common sense or wisdom. This last phrase '⊠⊠⊠⊠⊠⊠⊠⊠⊠ ⊠⊠⊠⊠⊠⊠⊠ ⊠⊠⊠⊠⊠?' is one of the most quoted expressions even in the modren times.]

बन्धानि खलु सन्ति बहूनि प्रेमरज्जुकृतबन्धनमन्यत्।
दारुभोदनिपुणोऽपि षडंघ्रि र्निष्क्रियो भवति पंकजकोशे ॥ 202 ॥

Bandhanaani Khalu Santi Bahooni Premarajjukritabandhanmannyat.
Daarubhedanipunoapi Shandanghrirniskriyo Bhvati Pankaj Koshe.

There are many a bondage but that of love is entirely different. The black bee which penetrates through even wood gets inertly enclosed in the fold of the lotus flower.

[This is again a very poetic observation of supreme order. Chanakya says that love mellows down the beloved as the black-bee, capable of penetrating through as hard the material as wood, lovingly allows itself to be enclosed in the soft fold of the lotus. Indeed the bond of love it unique!]

स्वहस्तग्रथिंता माला स्वहस्तघृष्टचंदनम्।
स्वहस्तलिखितस्तोत्रां शक्रस्यापि श्रियं हरेत् ।। 203 ।।

Svahastagranthitaa Maala Svahastaagtirishtachandanam.
Svahastalikhitastottram Shakrassyaapi Shriyam Haret.

The self-kneaded garland (of flowers), the self rubbed sandalwood (paste) and the self-created stotra denude even the chief of the god Indra of the graceful charm.

[One should never wear a garland made by oneself and should never apply the sandal paste rubbed by oneself as doing so takes away the charm. Similarly, one should never sing the self¬-created hymn. This observation stresses the obvious. In other words, it expresses the same feeling that 'self-praise is no recommendation'.]

गुहासक्तस्य नो विद्या न दया मांसभोजनः।
दुव्य लुब्धस्य नो सत्यं न स्त्रौणस्य पवित्राता ।। 204।।

Grihaasaktassya No Viddyaa Na dayaa Maansabhojinah.
Dravya Lubdhassya Sattyam Na Strainassya Pavitrataa.

One who is attached to home does not get knowledge (education), meat-eaters are not merciful; greedy are not veridical and effeminates are not pure.

[Those who do not wish to get out of their homes cannot hope to be wise because they restrict their life to the confines of home. It is believed that knowledge is exposure to life. If one doesn't expose oneself, how he is likely to become wise? The variety of experience adds to one's knowledge. Obviously, a homing pigeon-type of man cannot be learned and knowledgeable. It is generally believed that those who eat meat have a killer's urge which dries their sense of mercy. Similarly, a greedy man cannot view anything with impartiality. Naturally, he would not be truthful.

An effeminate person lacks firmness and will. Such boneless persons are ready for any compromise. And a compromising person can accept compromise at any level, whether physical or mental. Purity, whether mental or physical is maintained by a firm adherence of certain principles. Here an effeminate man doesn't literally mean a man behaving as a woman but someone with a very weak will.]

कोऽर्थान्प्राप्य न गर्वितो विषयिण: कस्यापदोस्तंगता: ।
स्त्रीभि: कस्य न खण्डितं भुवि: मन: को नाम राज्ञप्रिय: ।।
क: कालस्य न गोचरत्वमगमत कोऽर्थीऽगतो गौरवम्।
को वा दुर्जनदुर्गुणेषु पतित: क्षेमेण यात: पथि ।। 205 ।।

Koarthannpraappya Na Garvito Vishyinah Kasyaapadoa stangataah
Streebhih Kasya Na Khanditam Bhuvih Manah Konaam Raagyapriyah.
Kah Kaalasya Na Gocharattvamgamat Koarthee Gato Gauravam
Ko Vaa durjan durguneshu Patitah Kshemen Yaatah Pathi.

Who doesn't grow arrogant by coming in riches? What could indulge in the sensual pleasures end one's grief? Whose heart has not been broken by women? Who could win the king's favour for ever? Who didn't bear the evil glance of time? Which beggar could ever command regard? Who is that person who could return safely after being trapped in the wickedness of the vile?

[These observations in the form of query stress the opposite like "who doesn't grow arrogant. . ." means riches make the receiver go arrogant certainly. Chanakya shared the inbuilt prejudice against women commonly prevalent in the ancient times, and hence the observation whose heart has not been broken by women.

The royal favours are proverbially fickle, no king could be favourable to anyone for long. The rest of the observations are self evident.]

निमंत्राणोत्सवा विप्रा गावो नव तृणेत्सवा।
पत्युत्साहयुता भर्या अहं कृष्ण रणोत्सव: ।। 206 ।।

Nimantranottsava vippraa Gaavo Nav Trinottsavaah.
Pattyuttsaahayutaa Bharyaa Aham Krishna Ranottsavah.

Invitation (for a feast) heralds the onset of a festival for a brahman; sprouting of the fresh grass for a cow; arrival of the husband (from the foreign strand) for the wife, and O Krishna! My festival is war.

[That is of the brave, the war heralds the onset of a festival.]

बहूनां चैव सात्वानां समवायो रिपुजय:।
वर्षान्धराध्रो मेघ्स्तृणैरपि निवार्यते ।। 207।।

Bahoonaam Chaiv Sattvaanaam Samavaayo Ripuujayah.
Varshaandhaaraadharo Meghastrinairapi Nivaaryate.

Many tiny beings, when combined, vanquish even a big enemy. The collective strength of the infinitiesimal straws prevent even the fierce rain-water from passing through them.

[Chanakya says that unity given us a big strength and helps us defeat our even bigger adversaries. A thatched hut is made of tiny straw bits. But when these straws are properly united, they prevent even the fieriest rain water from passing through them.]

> जलविन्दुनिपातेन क्रमशः पूर्यते घटः।
> स हेतु सर्वविद्यानां धर्मस्य च धनस्य च ।। 208 ।।

Jalvindunipaaten Kramashah Pooryate Ghatah.
Sahetu Sarvaviddyaanaam Dhardasya Cha Dhanasya Cha.

A mere trickle of the tiny drops of water can-fill the pitcher. The same way we must keep on collecting knowledge, Dharma and money.

[We should not neglect even the tiniest fraction of useful knowledge whose treasure become great when collected even in bits. The same way we must go on accruing the merit by upholding our religious or moral tenets and by being fair to all. This is how we must go on collecting the wealth and riches. It is these tiny trickle which eventually become the massive reservoirs.]

> धनेषु जीवितव्येषु स्त्रीषु चाहारकर्मषु।
> अतृप्ता प्राणिनः सर्वेयाता यास्यन्ति यान्ति च ।। 209 ।।

Dhaneshu Jeevitavyeshu Streeshu Chahaarakarmeshu.
Atriptaa Praaninah Sarve Yaataa Yaasyanti Yaanti Cha.

All beings have left, are leaving and shall leave this world totally dissatisfied with whatever they have received, are receiving and shall receive in the form of wealth, life, woman and food.

[Chanakya says that sensual cravings knows no satisfaction for they tend to grow on what they are fed. With the result that no one could ever be satisfied with whatever wealth one may have earned, the span of life one may have lived, the woman (or women) and food one may have enjoyed.]

दातृत्वं प्रियवक्तृत्वं धीरत्वमुचितज्ञता।
अभ्यासेन न लभ्यंते चत्वार: सहजा गुणा ।। 210 ।।

Daatritvam Priyavaktrittvam Dheerattvamuchitagyateaa.
Abhyaasen Na Labhyante Chattvaarah Sahajaa Gunaa.

Charitable disposition, sweet tongue, patience and proper wisdom (according to the, demands of the occasion) are the inborn properties of a person which cannot be cultivated by practice.

[Charity, patience, world wiseness are the natural qualities, they can't be inculcated by any amount of practice.]

धनिक: श्रोत्रियो राजा नदी वैद्यस्तु पचम: ।
पञ्च यत्र न विद्यन्ते न तत्र दिवसे वसेत ।। 211।।

Dhanikah Shrotriyo Raajaa Nadee Vaiddyastu Panchamah.
Pancha Yatra Na Viddyante Tatra Divase Vaset.

One shouldn't stay at a place where there be no seth (rich man to dole out money if the need be), a scholar well versed in the Vedas (to clear any confusion regarding what one should do and what one shouldn't), a King (or some one in authority to enforce law and order), a Vaidya (or physician to help one in case of any ailment) and a river (to meet one's need for water) even for a day.

लोकयात्रा भयं लज्जा दाक्षिण्यं त्यागशीलता।
पच यत्रा न विद्यन्ते न कुर्यात्तत्रा संगतिम् ।। 212 ।।

Lokayaatraa Bhayam Lajjaa Dakshinnyam Tyaagasheelataa.
Panch Yatra Na Vidyante Kuryattatra Sangtim.

Where there be no possibility of earning one's livelihood; where people be devoid of fear, shame, charity and magnanimity–one should not have any attachment for such five place.

[i.e. one should not think of dwelling at such places. The fear here referred to is for the fear of the social norms or law in whose absence people invariably grow anarchic and delinquent. The other points are self evident.]

यस्मिन देशे न सम्मानो न वृत्तिर्न च बान्ध्वाः।
न य विद्यागमोऽप्यस्ति वासस्तत्र न कारयेत ।। 213 ।।

Yassmin Deshe Na Sammano Na Vrittirna Cha Baandhavah.
Na Ya Viddyaagamoappyasti Vaasastatra Na Kaaryet.

One shouldn't at a place where one may not receive any respect (of the people); Where there may not be any possibility of earning one's livelihood; where one may not have any close relation living already there and where there may not be any chance of enhancing one's knowledge (or getting good education.)

यो ध्रुवाणि परित्यज्य ह्यध्रुवं परिसेवते।
ध्रुवाणि तस्य नश्यन्ति चाध्रुवं नष्टमेव हि ।। 214 ।।

Yo Dhruvaani Parityajjya Hyadhruvam Parisevate.
Dhruvaani Tassya Mashyanti Chaadhruvam Nashtamev Hi.

He who forgoes the certain for the uncertain has his certain also destroyed. The uncertain even otherwise would be destroyed on its own.

[The aphorism conveys, the same meaning as conveyed by the famous English proverb: 'One in hand is better than two in the bush'.]

परोक्षे कार्यहन्तारं प्रत्यक्षे प्रियवादिनम्।
वर्जयेत्तादृशं मित्रां विषकुम्भं पयोमुखम् ।। 215 ।।

Parokshe Kaaryahantaaram Prattyakshe Priyavaadinam.
Varjayettadrisham Mittram Vishkumbham Payomukham.

Shun a friend speaking fair on the face but acting foul in the absence like the pitcher filled with venom but having milk at the opening. [It means shun contact with an insincere friend who does good only to hoodwink you, for such a friend is no friend at all.]

नदीनां शस्त्रापाणीनां नखीनां श्रृंगिणां तथा।
विश्वासो नैव कर्तव्य: स्त्रीषु राजकुलेषु च ।। 216 ।।

Nadeenaam Shastrapaaneenaam Nakheenaam Shringinaam Tathaa.
Vishwaaso Naiv Kartavyah Streeshu Rajuleshu Cha.

Rivers, weapon-weilders (having weapon in their hands), animals (beasts) with horn and paws, women and the members of the royal family should never be taken for granted.

[One should never attempt to cross the river without

assessing its depth and width, its current strength, etc. Similarly, those having weapon in their hand should never be taken for granted, for even the slightest suggestion of the provocation is enough to make them use their weapon. He has no preparation to make, the weapon is already in his hand. The same is true with the animals with horn and paws-a little carelessness can make them damage you. Lastly, women and the royal personages are fickle by their nature; hence one can't be sure about their behaviour. Those who take these for granted suffer the adverse consequences.]

न विश्वसेत्कुमित्रो च मित्रो चापि न विश्वसेत्।
कदाचित्कुपितं मित्रां सर्व गुह्यं प्रकाशयेत् ।। 217 ।।

Na Vishuaset Kumitre Cha Mitre Chaapina Vishvaset.
Kadaachittkupitam Mitram Sarva Gurhyaim Prakshyet.

Never trust even your good friend, let alone the vile one, in anger your friend can expose your secrets out of vengence.

[Chanakya doesn't advise fully trusting even your best friend. There are certain secrets in one's life which should never be discussed with anyone, even with your best friend who might embarrass you by exposing them in a fit of rage.]

अर्थनाश मनस्तापं गृहिण्याश्चरितानि च।
नीचं वाक्यं चापमानं मतिमानन प्रकाशयेत ।। 218 ।।

Arthanaash Manastaapapapam Grihnyaashcharitaani Cha.
Neechamvaakyam Chaapamaanam Matimaann Prakaashyet.

Prudence lies in not disclosing to anyone the following secret: loss of one's wealth; some personal tragedy; suspicion on wife's conduct; mean outpourings of a vile person and the personal ignominy. [This observation is actually the continuation of the earlier one. In this, Chanakya spells out the secrets that shouldn't be disclosed to anyone, for their disclosure would adds to one's distress or discomfiture without providing any relief whatsoever.]

मनसा चिन्तितं काय वचसा न प्रकाशयेत्।
मन्त्रेण रक्षयेद्द गूढं कार्य चापि नियोजनयेत् ।। 219 ।।

Manasaa Chintitam Kaaryam Vachsaa Na Prakaashyet.
Mantren Rakshnyed goodham kaaryam Chaapi Niyojayet.

One should never leak out one's well-thought out intentions, determinations and they should be jealously guarded like some secret Mantra. The implementation of them should also be achieved without any fanfare and in total secrecy (to ensure their successful accomplishment.)

[Immature exposure of one's intention often brings failure in its trail. If one has deliberated well on doing some particular job, it is only the total secrecy which ensures one's applying one's full potential in implementing them successfully.]

लालनाद्द बहवो दोषास्ताडनाद्द बहवो गुणा:।
तस्मात्पुत्रां च शिष्यं च ताडयेनन तु लालयेत् ।। 220 ।।

Laalanaad Bahavo Doshaastaadanaad Bahavo Gunaah.
Tasmaatputtram Cha Shishyam Cha Tadayenn Tu Laalyet.

Excessive affection breeds flaws and admonition good qualities. Hence one's son and disciple need more of admonition and less of affection.

[This stage obviously comes when the son or the disciple is a little grown up, i.e. when they are prone to a variety of distraction and deviation from their aim out of the curiousity unchecked by discertion. This stage comes after the child is out of infancy and about to enter the stage of adolescence: Constant admonition would make him keep his energies totally applies to his marked pursuit.]

पादशेषं पीतशेषं सान्यशेषं तथैव च।
श्वानमूत्रासमं तोयं पीत्वा चान्द्रायणं चरेत् ।। 221 ।।

Paadshesham Peetashesham Saandhyashesham Tathaiv Cha.
Shvanamootrasamam Toyam Peettvaa Chandraayanam Charet.

The leftover water after washing one's feet, drinking to one's need and after completing the Sandhya Worship (worship conducted in the morning and evening, during the transitional phase of night to day and vice versa) should never be consumed as if is as abhorsome as the urine of dog. If one drinks it, one must perform the fast of Chandrayan.

[The crux of the aphorism is that water one used should never be used purely from the hygienic point of view. In a hot and humid climate, even water gets polluted when used. Moreover, the aphorism is also guided by the abundance of water. This could not have been an observation of an Arabic thinker where in his country where water is the most precious commodity, but only of an ancient North Indian whose land had abundant water supply. Chandrayan Vrat means keeping fast the whole day and having food and water only after seeing the moon.]

प्रियोर्विप्रवहेश्च दम्पत्योः स्वामिभृत्ययोः।
अन्तरेण न गन्तव्यं हलस्य वृषभस्य च ॥ 222 ॥

Vipprayorvipprávhaneshcha Dampattyoh Swamibhrittyoyh.
Antaren Nagantawyam Halasya Vrishabhasya Cha.

Never pass through between the two brahmans; between fire and a brahman; between the master and the servant; between the husband and wife; and between the plough and the bullocks.

पादाभ्यां न स्पृशंदग्निं गुरुं ब्राह्मणमेव च।
नैव गावं कुमारीं चन न वृद्धं न शिशुं तथा ॥ 223 ॥

Paadaabhyam Na Sprashandagnint Gurum Brahmanmeva Cha.
Naiv Gaavam Kumarim Cha Na Vriddham Na Shishum Tathaa.

Never touch the fire, the guru, the brahman, the cow, the maiden girl, the old people and the kids. It is ill-mannerly to do so.

उत्पन्नपश्चात्तापस्य बुद्धिर्भवति यादृशी।
तादृशी यदि पूर्व स्यात्कस्य स्यान्न महोदयः ॥ 224 ॥

Uttpannapashchaataapassya Buddhirbhavati Yaadrishee.
Taadrishee Yadi Poorva Syaatkasya Syaanna Mahodayah.

One repents after committing a mistake but if one gets such a wisdom before committing a mistake one's progress cannot be stalled.

[A wrong act entails repentance. One gets remorseful after knowing the fault he has committed. But if he could be wise enough before committing the act, there is no going back for him; for if one acts after carefully brooding on his course of action, there is no set back and hence the progress is unchecked and speedy.]

> **त्यचेदेकं कुलस्यार्थे ग्रामस्यार्थे कुलं त्यजेत्।**
> **ग्रामं जनपदस्यार्थे आत्मार्थे पृथिवीं त्यजत् ।। 225 ।।**

Tyajedekam Kulasyaarthe Graamassyaarthe Kulam Tyajet.
Graamam Janapadasyaarthe Aattmaarthe Prithiveem Tyajat.

Sacrifice a person for the sake of the family, a family for a village, a village for the state but for the self the entire world.

[This oft-quoted shloka shows the degree of importance of an entity: of a person vis-a-vis a family; of a family vis-a-vis a village; of a village vis-a-vis a state; of the world vis-a-vis the self. In short the self protection is deemed paramount but here the self doesn't mean only the selfish interest, it means the dictates of the inner conscience which ought to be held supreme.]

> **आपदर्थ धनं रक्षेद दारान रक्षेद धनैरपि।**
> **आत्मानं सततं रक्षेद दारैरपि ध्नैरपि ।। 226 ।।**

Aapadartham Dhanam Rakshed Daaraan RAkshed Dhanairapi.
Aatmaanam Satatam Rakshd Daarairapi Dhanairapi.

Protect riches (money) at the time of distress but protect wife (spouse) more than money and oneself more the riches and wife.

[This Sholka again shows the degree of importance at the time of distress: self, spouse and riches in that order. Self is given the maximum importance because riches, wife and other 'musts' are useful only when one survives. Hence the importance.]

जानीयात्प्रेषणेभृत्यान् बान्धवानव्यसगनागमे।
मित्रं चापत्तिकालेषु भाया च विभवक्षये ।। 227।।

Jaaneeyaatpreshanebhrittyaan Baandhavaanvyasanaagame.
Mitram Chaapiattikaaleshu Bhaaryaam Cha Vibhavakshaye.

The servant is tested when he is sent on an important mission, the Kith and Kin are tested in one's own distress, a friend at the hour of need or emergency and the wife when one loses one's wealth.

यस्य बुद्धिर्बलं तस्य निर्बुद्धेस्तु कुतो बलम्।
वने सिंहो ममदोन्मत: शाशकेन निपातित: ।। 228 ।।

Yasyabuddhirbalam Tassya Nirbuddhestu Kuto Balam.
Vane Singho Mamadonmattah Shashaken Nipaatitah.

He who has intelligence has power, for how can a fool has any power? A tiny rabbit is capable of slaying even a charged lion in the Jungle.

[Intelligence scores over mere physical power. It is because of this mental shrewdness that a tiny rabbit is able to slay even a charged lion. This observation is derived from the old tale in which a tiny rabbit fools a mighty lion and manages to let the lion fall in a blind well and die. This tale is so symbolical that lion's different forms is found in a score of ancient books of many countries.]

हस्ती स्थूलतनु: स चांकुशवशं: किं हस्तिमात्रोंऽकुश:
दीपे प्रज्वलिते प्रणश्यति तम: किं दीपमात्रं तम:।
वज्रेणाभिहता: पतन्ति गिरय: किं व्रज्रमात्रां नगा:
तेजो यस्य विराजते स बलवान स्थूलेषु क: प्रत्यय: ।। 229 ।।

Hastee sthooltanuh sa Chankushuashah Kim Hastimaatronkushah
Deepe Prajjvalite Pranashyati Tamah Kim Deepamaatram Tamah.
Vajjrenabhhihataah Patanti Giryaah Kim Vijjramaatram Nagaah
Tejo Yasya Viraajate Sa Balvaan Sthooleshu Kah Prattyayah.

Despite being of a massive body an elephant is controlled by the goad. Does that make the goad as powerful as the elephant? A lamp when kindled removes darkness-does that makes the lamp equal to the darkness? The blows of a thunderbolt breaks a mountain into pieces.¬ Does that make the thunderbolt as big as a mountain? No. The brilliance has the power, physical massiveness does not matter.

[Chanakya stresses the need of sharpness of the brain and intelligence against physical power. He says the brain always scores over brawn, which is a universal fact. Quoting various examples from nature, he proves his point quite poetically.]

बलं विद्या च विप्राणां राज्ञ: सैन्यं बलं तथा।
बलं वित्तं च वैश्यानां शूद्राणां च कनिष्ठता ।। 230 ।।

Balam Viddyaacha Vipraanaam Raagyaah Sainnyam Balam Tathaa.
Balam Vittam Cha Vaishyaanaam Shoodraanaam Cha Kanishthataa.

The power of the brahmans is knowledge, of the king his army, of the trader-class their wealth and of the menial class their service ability. [Chanakya here stresses the truism first ennunciated by Manu.]

बाहुवीय बलं राजा ब्राह्मणो ब्रह्मवितद्‌ बली।
रूपयौवनमाधुय स्त्रीणां बलमुत्तमम ।। 231 ।।

Baahveeryam Balam Raajaa Brahamno Bramhvid Balee.
Roopyauvanmaadhuryam Streenaam Balmuttamam.

The mighty-armed king is powerful; the power of the brahmans lies in their capacity to realise the Brahm {the ultimate}, beauty, youth and comeliness constitute the power of the ladies.

[That king is deemed to be really powerful of the ladies. Who possesses the fount of his strength in his own self i.e., he doesn't depend upon any other authority to weiled his power. The power, brilliance or ability of a brahman is judged by his capacity to realise the ultimate god, which means he must lead an austeric self-controlled and totally devoted life in the worship of God. The fount of a woman's strength lies naturally in her beauteous form, youthful appearance and sweet, comely mannerism.]

नात्यन्तं सलेन भाव्यं गत्वा पश्य वनस्थलीम्।
छिद्यन्ते सरलास्तत्रा कुब्जास्तिष्ठन्ति पादपा: ।। 232 ।।

Naattyantam Saralen Bhaavyam Gattvaa Pashya Vanasthaleem.
Chiddyante Saralaastatra Kubjaastishthanti Paadapaah.

One should never be too simple. If one goes to the jungle one beholds that the simple, straight trees have been cut but those which grow in a haphazard manner are spared.

[A man should be simple hearted, straight mannered but not a simpletion. Or he is subject to the constant exposure of being granted and they suffer in the conequece out of their simplicity. Giving the example of trees, he says that mostly one is exploited for one's generosity. If you are rude in behaviour and harsh in tongue; you, might be spreaded like those trees which grow in a wild manner.]

अति रूपेण वै सीता चातिगर्वेण रावणः।
अतिदानाद् बलिर्बद्धो ह्यति सर्वत्रा वर्जयेत् ।। 233 ।।

Atiroopen Vai Seetaa Chaatigarvena Raavanah.
Atiddanaad Balirbaddho Hayati Sarvatra Varjayet.

The excessive beauty caused Sita to be eloped, the excessive arrogance caused Ravan's slaughter and excessive charitable disposition cause the king Bali to be duped. Hence excess is bad everywhere.

[First two -references are quite well known. The king Bali was the famous demon king who was deceived by Lord Vishnu himself in the Vaman form. Chanakya says even the good qualitiesbecomes bad in excess, let alone the bad ones. Excess of everything is bad.]

उद्योगो नास्ति दारिद्रयं जपतो नास्ति पातकम्।
मौनने कहो नास्ति जाग्रतस्य च न भयम ।। 234 ।।

Udyogo Naasti Daridaryan Japato Naasti Patakam.
Maunane Kaho Naasti Jagratasya Cha Na Bhayam.

Enterprise vanishes poverty and the chanting (of Mantra or God's name) dissipates sin. Silence ends embroilment and awakening removes fear.

उपसर्गेऽन्यचक्रे च दुर्भिक्षे च भयावहे।
असाधुजनसम्पर्के पलायति स जीवति ।। 235 ।।

Upasargeannyachakre Cha Durbhikshe Cha Bhayaavahe.
Asaddhu Jansamparke Palaayati Sa jeevati.

He who manages to escape from riots or scuffles, from the severe draught or from the evil company survives.

(Meaning that no one should stay at such places where riots, scuffles, severe drought or evil company be disturbing the area.)

तावद् भयेषु भेतव्यं यावद् भयमनागतम्।
आगतं तु भयं वीक्ष्य प्रहर्तव्यशंकया ।। 236 ।।

Taavad Bhayeshu Bhetavyam Yaadav Bhayamanaagatam.
Aagatam Tu Bhayam Veekshaya Prahartavyamshankayaa.

One should be apprehensive of the cause of fear till it is far off, but when it comes close, fight it undaunted.

[This is a natural human psychology that we apprehend the danger till it is far off. When it comes close the only way to deal, with it is to take on with total might, for in that stage the apprehension vanishes. Chanakya also confirms that this is the only way to overcome the fear.]

अनुलोमेन बलिनं प्रतिलोमेन दुर्जनम।
आत्मतुल्यबलं शत्रुं विनयेन बलेन वा ।। 237 ।।

Anulomen Balinam Pratilomen Durjanam.
Aatmatullyambalam Shatrum Vinayen Balen Vaa.

Deal with the powerful enemy by trying to win its favour (as a part of the strategy), with the wicked enemy by going away and with the enemy of matching power by being submissive or aggressive as the situation may demand. Direct opposition of the powerful enemy will cause sure defeat. In that case, it is always prudent to avoid direct confrontation. Trying to win favour means keeping him confused of your intention. If the enemy is wicked you never know what he might be upto. It is always better to avoid him and seize your opportunity to smash him in the least blows possible. It is only against an enemy of the matching power that one has to be aggressive or submissive according to the demand of the situtation.

वरं न राजा न कुराजराजा
वरं न मित्रां न कुमित्रामित्राम्।
वरं न शिष्यो न कुशिष्यशिष्य: ।। 238 ।।

Varam Na Raaja Na Kuraajaraajaa
Varam Na Mitram Na Kumitramitram.
Varam Na Shishyo Na Kushishyashishyah
Varam Na Daaraa Na Kudaaradaaraah.

It is better not to have a king than have a king who is tyrant; not to` have a friend than have a wicked friend; not to have a wife than have an unfaithful wife.

[A tyrant king, a wicked friend, a bad disciple and an unfaithful wife should not be acceptable. It is better to go without them, as in such cases their absence ensures more peace and happiness than their presence.]

कुराजराज्येन कुत: प्रजासुखं
कुमित्रामित्रोण कुतोभिनिवृत्ति:।
कुदारदारैश्च कुतो गृहे रति:
कुशिष्यमयापयत: कुतो यश: ॥ 239 ॥

Kuraajraajjyen Kutah Prajaasakham
Kumitramitren Kutoabhinivrittih.
Kudaaradaaraishcha Kuto Grihe Ratih
Kushishyamaddhyaaapayatah Kuto Yashah.

How can the subjects be happy in the rule of a tyrant king? How can one get happiness in the company of a wicked friend? How can one enjoy domestic bliss with an unfaithful wife? And what renown can one earn by teaching a bad disciple.

[This Shloka is almost the extention of the previous Shloka. In this, Chanakya specifies the situation resulting out of getting a tyrant king, a wicked friend, the unfaithful wife and a pad disciple.]

गृहीत्वा दक्षिणां विप्रास्तयजन्ति यजमानकम्।
प्राप्तविद्या गुरुं शिष्या दग्धरण्यं मृगास्तथा ॥ 240 ॥

Griheettvaa Dakshinaam Vippraasttyajanti Yajmanakam.
Praaptaviddyaa Gurum Shishyaah Daggdhaarannyam Mrigaastathaa.

The brahmans leave their host after getting the honorarium; the disciple leave their teacher after receiving education; the beasts leave the jungle when fire breaks out there.

[This is a pithy yet melancholic observation. Chanakya says that driven by the matter of fact and selfish consideration all stay with anyone till they receive some material benefit. This is the golden rule of a materialistic world. A brahman stays with the host till he receives his honorarium. Similarly, students desert their teacher after getting education. Even the wild beasts, who feed on the luscious bounty of the jungle desert it when it comes to distress with the outbreak of the jungle fire. All are basically selfish.]

> निर्धन पुरुषं वेश्या प्रजा भग्नं नृपं त्यजेत्।
> शास्त्रापूतं वदेद्‌ वाक्यं मन:पूतं समाचरेत् ।। 241 ।।

Nirdhanam Purusham Veshyaa Prajaa Bhagnam Nripam Tyajet.
Khagaah Veetphalam Vriksham Bhuktvaa Chaabhyagato Griham.

The prostitute deserts a poor customer, the subjects desert a powerless king. The same way thebirds desert a fruitless tree and the guest deserts the host-house after having his food.

[Continuing with the previous observation, Chanakya says that all stay till they receive benefits? then all desert– the prostitute, a poor customer, the subjects, a powerless king, the birds, a fruitless tree, and the guest, his host's house, after filling his belly. All stay to serve their purpose without caring for the benefactor's need.]

> दृष्टिपूतं न्यसेत् पादं वस्त्रापूतं जल पिवेत्।
> शास्त्रापूतं वदेद्‌ वाक्यं मन:पूतं समाचरेत् ।। 242 ।।

Drishtipootam Nyaset Paadam Vastrapootam Jalam Pibet.
Shaastrapootam Veded Vaakyam Manahpootam Samaacharet.

One should step forward after fully viewing the path, drink water after straining it through a (clean) cloth; talk in conformity with the scriptural dIctates and act according to what one's conscience allows.

[These are ancient safety measures which are still quite relevant in their essential message.]

स्वभावेन हि तुष्यन्ति देवा: सत्पुरुषा पिता।
ज्ञातय: स्नानपानाभ्यां वाक्यदानेन पण्डिता: ।। 243 ।।

Svabhaaven Hitushyanti Devaah Satpurushah Pitaa.
Gyaatayaah Snaapaanaabhyaam Vaakyadaanen Panditaah.

Gods, noble persons and father are pleased by one's behaviour; other kith and kin by enjoying food and drink (together) and the scholars by the sweet speech.

अनभ्यासे विषं शास्त्राजीर्णे भोजनं विषम्।
दरिद्रस्य विषं गोष्ठी वृद्धस्य तरुणी विषम् ।। 244।।

Anabhyaase Visham Shaastramjeerne Bhojanam Visham.
Daridasya Visham Goshthee Vriddhassya Tarunee Visham.

Lack of practice makes the learning a poison; indigestion makes food a poison; conferences breed venom for the poor and a young woman is poisonous for an old man.

[Any learning or expertise if not put to proper practice acts like poison. And even nectar can turn into poison if your digestion is weak because it is only after the food is digested that our body derives the required nourishment. Poverty is such a condition where no one wants to advertise or make others know about one acute indigence.

Since the conferences exposes this condition to so many persons, they do breed venom for such a man. And lastly, young woman is a poison for an old man because in the old age the sexual appetite remains but due to the physical ennervation the performance become impossible. But on getting a young woman, the old persons would make their bodies overexert to achieve the desired performance. This over exertion may lead to death if not checked. Hence a young woman is poison for an old man.]

स्पृहो नाध्किारी स्यात्र कामी भण्डनप्रिया।
नो विदग्ध: प्रियं बूयात् स्पष्ट वक्ता न वंचक: ।। 245 ।।

Nispriho Naadhikaaree Syaanna Kaamee Bhandampriyaa.
No Vidagdhah Priyam Brooyaat Spashta Vaktaa Na Vanchakah.

A hermit is no authority on any subject; one who is not lecherous doesn't need to decorate oneself; the scholars, seldom speak sweetly and the straight-forward, outspoken man is never a thug.

[A hermit is a man who has renounced the world due to the aversion he felt for the material things. How can he, then, know about anything about the world? One decorates and gets make-up only to attract the opposite sex. When lacking in that urge, the desire to decorate oneself does not arise. The scholars are those who, due to their learning, see the reality much more clearly than others. And since reality is always bitter, how can they speak sweetly? Lastly, one who is not able to hide his true feeling can not hide his vile intentions also if he has them. But for thuggery or chicanery what needed is secrecy. Obviously, thuggery and outspokenness are not compatible.]

नास्ति मेघसमं तोयं नास्ति चात्मसमं बलम्।
नास्ति चक्षुसमं तेजो नास्ति चात्रसमं प्रियम् ।। 246 ।।

Naasti Meghasamam Toyam Naasti Chuatsamam Balam.
Naasti Chakshusaman Tejo Naasti Chaannsam Priyam.

Clouds are the best source of water; self-strength is the best power, eyes are the best light and cereal (food) is the best desired object.

[Since clouds carry the water to the most remote area and they bring water when most needed, they give us the best water–the best is what you need most at the most distressing situation. Self-strength is the most reliable power, hence best power. Every light is useless if one can't see or if one has no eyes. Hence the eyes give us the best light. And no being can exist without food, hence food is the most desired object.]

कस्य दोषः कुले नास्ति व्याध्रिा को न पीडितः।
व्यसनं केन न प्राप्तं कस्य सौख्यं निरन्तरम् ।। 247 ।।

Kassya Doshah Kule Naasti Vyaadhinaa Ko Na Peeditah.
Vyhasanam Kenna Praaptam Kasya Saukhyam Nirantaram.

Whose family is blemishless? Who is not troubled by diseases? Who dosen't suffer grief and who is perpetually happy.

[All these observations are based on the bitter facts which say that grief and misery are the part and parcel of the human existence in the world.]

राजा राष्ट्रकृतं पापं राज्ञः पापं पुरोहितः।
भर्ता च स्त्रीकृतं पापं शिष्य पाप गुरुस्तथा ।। 248 ।।

Raajaa Raashtrakritam Paapam Raagyah Paapam Purohitah.
Bhartaa Cha Streekritam Paapam Shishya Paap Gurustathaa.

The king suffers the consequences of the sin committed by a nation (State), the king's sins are suffered by his priest, the wife's sins are suffered by the husband, and that of the disciple by the guru.

[Since the king has the responsibility of running the State or the nation, naturally he can't escape the consequence if someone has committed sins in his State. And the king is supposed to rule by the advice of his priest. So for king's fault, the priest can't escape blame. Similarly, the wife's sins have to be suffered by the husband who is responsible for her, and similarly, of the disciple by the Guru.]'

यस्मिन् रुष्टे भयं नास्ति तुष्टे नैव धागमः।
निग्रहोऽनुग्रहो नास्ति स रुष्टः किं करितष्यति ।। 249 ।।

Yasmin Rushte Bhayam Naasti Tushte Naiv Dhanaagamah.
Nigrahoanugraho Naasti Sarushtah Kim Karishyati.

He whose wrath causes no fear and happiness gives no money who neither can punish anyone nor show his favour–the anger of such a person is of no consequence.

[The truth in the observation is selfevident. Totally inconcious or ineffective person is of no consequence in the society.]

कवयः किं न पश्यन्ति किं न कुव्रन्ति योषितः।
मद्यपा किं न जल्पन्ति किं न खादन्ति वायसाः ।। 250 ।।

Kavayah kim Na Pashyanti Kimna Kurvanti Yoshitah.
Maddyapaa Kimna Jalpanti Kim Na Khaadanti Vaayasaah.

What is that which the poets do not see? What is that which

the woman cannot do? What is that which the drunkards do not babble and what is that which is not eaten by the crows?

[Poets in their imagination can reach everywhere hence nothing is left unseen by them. Figuratively, women are capable of doing the most babble and the meanest deed possible, hence no holds are barred for them. A drunkard can mouth the filthiest abuse and for them also there is no limit on the either side. Similarly, the crows do not make any distinction in their choice of food and can devour even the dirtiest object.]

नैव पश्यति जन्मानधः कामान्धे नैव पश्यति।
मदोन्मत्ता न पश्यन्ति अर्थी दोषं न पश्यति ।। 251 ।।

Naiv Pashyanti Janmandhah Kaamaandho Naiv Pashyanti.
Madonmatta Na Pashyanti Arthee Dosham Na Pashyanti.

A born-blind man cannot see anything; the persons blinded by their sexual desire or sozzled with the intoxication cannot see anything. Similarly, a man blinded by his need cannot perceive any flaw in the desired object.

अशक्तस्तुभवेत्साधुर्ब्रह्मचारी च निर्धनः।
व्याधिष्ठो देवभक्तश्च वृद्धा नारी पतिव्रता ।। 252 ।।

Ashaktastubhavetsaadhurbrahmachaari Cha Nirdhanah.
Vyaadhishtho Devabhaktasheha Vriddha Naari Pativrataa.

A powerless man takes to the saffron robes; a pauper takes the vow celibacy, a diseased man becomes an ardent devotee (of God) and an old woman adheres to the most pious wifely vows.

[Meaning all seek these positions in their utter helplessness when they have no other alternative.]

अलिरयं नलिनिदलमयम: कमलिनीमकरन्दमदालस:।
विधिवशात्प्रदेशमुपागत: कुरजपुष्परसं बहु मन्यते ॥ 253 ॥

Alirayam Nalinidalamadhyama Kamalaneemakarandamadaalasah. Vidhivashaatpradeshmupaagatah Kurajpushparasam Bahu Mannyate.

This bee used to dwell among the lotus-petals and survived on imbibing the sap of the flowers. For some reason, it had to come to the foreign strand and now it regards a great gift to even the juice of the Kuruj flower.

[When dwelling among the lotus-petals, the bee considered even the sap of the lotus to be an ordinary thing. But when, due to some reason, it has to go away to the foreign strands, it began to deem even the Kuruj-flower-sap to be a great gift, i.e., when someone belonging to a high and rich family falls on evil days, he realises the importance of the past pleasures and compromises with existing fallen standard of living. Helplessness makes one regard even the common place or even inferior things as the great gifts.]

निर्विषेणाऽपि सर्पेण कर्तव्या महती फणा।
विषमस्तु न वाप्यस्तु घाटाटोपो भयंकर: ॥ 254 ॥

Nirvishenaapi Sarpena Kartavyaa Mahatee Phanaa. Vishamastu Na Vaappyastu Ghataatopo Bhayankarah.

Even if the snake be non-poisonous, it must spread its hood to the full. Whether it contains poison or not, it must spread its hood to frighten the people.

[Merely, by looking one can't know whether the snake is

poisonous or not but when it spreads its hood, this gesture is enough to frighten the people– meaning, for happy survival in a society, one must affect deterrant ostentation in one's behaviour to keep unwanted people at bay.]

त्यजेद्धर्म दयाहीनें विद्याहीनं गुरुं त्यजेत्।
त्यजेत्क्रोधमुखी भार्यं निःस्नेहान्बान्धवांस्त्यजेत् ।। 255 ।।

Tyajedharam Dayaaheenam Viddyaaheenam Gurum Tyajet.
Tyajettkrodhamukhi Bharyaam Nihshehaanbaandhavaansyajet.

Give up the faith devoid of compassion; the Guru devoid of knowledge, an irascible wife and relations devoid of affection.

[Faith, which is devoid of compassion is no faith; the Guru, who is devoid of knowledge is no guru; a wife devoid of good manners is no wife and the relations devoid of affection are no relations, hence they ought to be left for good.]

नदीतीरे च ये वृक्षाः परगृहेषु कामिनी।
मन्त्रिहीनाश्च राजनः शीघ्रं नश्यन्त्यसंशयम् ।। 256 ।।

Nadeeteere Chaaje Vrikshaah Pargriheshu Kaaminee.
Mantreeheenaashcha Raajanah Sheeghram Nashyanttyasanshayam.

The trees growing at the bank of the river, the woman staying in someone else's house and the king denuded of the cabinet (ministers) perish soon.

[The trees on the bank of a river are on infirmer land and face the danger of being taken away by flood waters. Also since the bodies are normally cremated on the bank of the rivers, the trees are likely to be cut for making the funeral pyre. Hence the trees on the river bank cannot last long. A woman staying in other's house cannot maintain her chastity and the firmness of her character for long and soon she will have to compromise. A king working without ministers does not get the right counsel and in this stage he is prone to committing a grave mistake causing his own downfall.]

अनालोच्य व्ययं कर्ता चानाथः कलहप्रियः।
आर्तः स्त्रीसर्वक्षेत्रोषु नरः शीघ्रं विनश्यति ।। 257 ।।

Anaalochya Vyayam Kartaa Chaanaathah Kalahapriyah.
Aartah Streesarvakshetreshu Narah Sheeghram vinashyati.

A man, recklessly spend-thrift, shelterless, cantankerous, coveting for women of every caste indiscriminately soon perishes.

[Obviously, such a man has no chance of faring in any different manner!]

आलस्योपहता विद्या परहस्तं गतं धनम्।
अल्पबीजहतं क्षेत्रां हतं सैन्यमनायकम् ।। 258 ।।

Aalasyopahataa Viddyaa Parahastam Gatam Dhanam.
Alpabeejahatam Kshetram Hatam Senyamanaayakam.

Callous lethargy destroys knowledge; others hold on your money soon destroys it for you; the field is destroyed by the lack of seed and the army is destroyed in the absence of a commander.

[A careless, lazy bloke cannot gain knowledge if he lacks in self-discipline which is a 'must' for becoming the learned. Money is with him who controls it. If others have control over it, deem it that it is lost for you. Lack of seed ruins the fertility of the field. It is a known fact that if you don't sow a field for years together, it turns barren. And how can an army fight without a cammander?]

दारिद्रयनाशनं दानं शीलं दुर्गतिनाशनम्।
अज्ञानतानाशिनी प्रज्ञा भावना भयनाशिनी ।। 259 ।।

Daariddrayahaashanam Daanam Sheelam Durgatinaashanam.
Agyaantaanaashinee Praygyaa Bhaavaanaa Bhayanaashinee.

Charity destroys poverty; right demeanour destroys distress; truth¬bearing wisdom destroys ignorance and the (determined) feeling destroys fear.

[Poverty means lack of resources and charity means giving help to others, which obviously gives the impression that the person has enough¬ for one doles out elms only when one has enough of everything. And when people learn that you are gifting things, they develop confidence in your financial worth and you start getting things on credit. Thus, your stock increases and soon you get rid of that poverty. If one can maintain one's balance, even in the severe distress, behave normally with total caution, the panic element in the distress vanishes. The same is true with other two observations. If one searches for the true knowledge, how can ignorance survive in one's thinking. And lastly, the sense of fear is based totally on your mental projection of a situation. In the dark, a tree might give impression of a ghost but if you have strong will you may go near the tree and see it to be nothing but a tree. That stage you can achieve even by mere feeling. Fear is the projected perception of a given situation which is not dependent upon the external factors. In fact, all the four observations are rooted in the psychological aspect of the human behaviour.]

हतं ज्ञानं क्रियाहीनं हतश्चाज्ञानतो नरः।
हतं निर्नायकं सैन्यं स्त्रियो नष्टा ह्यभर्तृका ॥ 260 ॥

Hatam Gyaanam Kriyaheenam Hatashchagyaanato Narah.
Hatam Nirnaayakam Sainnyaam Striyo Nashta Hayabatrikaa.

That knowledge which is not used gets destroyed. Ignorance destroys the man. An army which has no commander gets destroyed and a woman without (the protection of) her husband gets destroyed.

[Almost the similar thought was expressed in the earlier pages, which is duly explained. Please refer to that aphorism for the explanation.]

असन्तुष्टा द्विजा नष्टाः सन्तुष्टाश्च महीभृतः।
सलज्जा गणिका नष्टानिर्लज्जाश्च कुलांगनाः ॥ 261॥

Asantushtaa Dvijaa Nashtaah Santushtaashcha Maheebhratah.
Salajjaa Ganikaa Nashtaanirjalajjashecha Kulaanganaah.

An unsatisfied brahman and a satisfied king perish. A shy prostitute and a shameless bride of a noble family perish.

[A brahman must not be covetous of the worldly possessions, if he does so, he can't follow his chosen path of acquiring more and more knowledge. But if a king gets satisfied with his expeditions and victory marches, he exposes himself to invasion by others. A prostitute's profession is such that if she is shy she will lose her clientele and her means of wherewithal. But in contradistinction, the bride of a noble family has to be shy and bashful to win everyone's respect. A shameless bride is not deemed a respectable woman.]

> निर्गुणस्य हतं रूपं दु:शीलस्य हतं कुलम्।
> असिद्धस्य हता विद्या अभोगस्य हतं धनम् ।। 262 ।।

Nirgunasya Hatam roopam Duhasheelasya Hatam Kulam.
Asiddhyassya Hataa Viddhyaa Abhogasya Hatam Dhanam.

Beauty of the virtueless, lineage of the wicked, knowledge of the undeserving, and wealth of the unenjoyer perish.

[Beauty without virtue is like body without soul–it is fey and can't last long. Knowledge of the undeserving is the most deadly weapon for self-destruction. If a noble family has just one black-sheep, it is enough to bring blot on the entire family. Like a rotten apple injures all its companion, so a wicked member destroys his entire family. Wealth is meant to be enjoyed; those who preserve and protect it without enjoying it, lose it eventually.]

> अन्नहीनो दहेद्राष्ट्रं मन्त्राहीनश्च ऋत्विज:।
> यजमान दांनहीनो नास्ति यज्ञसमो रिपु:।। ।। 263 ।।

Annaheeno Dahedraashtram Mantraheenasheha Rittvijah.
Yajmaan Daanheeno Nassti Yagyasamo Ripuh.

A foodless state destroys its ruler, so do the brahmans assigned to perform yagya but without any knowledge of the Mantra and the host who doesn't pay the honorarium to the guest brahmans. To employ such brahmans for performing the sacrifice and allowing such a person to play host is tentamount committing an act of treason.

[Lack of food is the most potent cause for the dethronement of a ruler as it is the ruler's foremost duty to provide food or food material to the subjects: Asking the unlearned brahmans to perform yagya is to invite trouble due to their ignorance, instead of propitiating the deities they might incur their wrath. And the greatest offender to the moral sense is to accept the services without paying the adequate honorarium or remuneration. Even if the brahmans be unlearned, if the host has invited them unknowingly, then he must pay their due. One who does so is the meanest person. The state where the ruler fails to arrange adequate food supply to his subjects, the unlearned brahmans are asked to perform the yagya and if they are not paid their due honorarium is destined to be destroyed.]

परस्परस्य मार्मणि ये भाषन्ते नराधमा: ।
ते एव विलयं यान्ति वल्मीकोदरसर्पवत् ।। 264 ।।

Parasparasya Marmaani Ye Bhaashante Naraadhamaah.
Te Evavilayam Yaanti Vallameekodar Sarpvat.

Those who disclose the mutual secret to others perish like a snake getting destroyed in its own cavity.

[Disclosure of the mutual secrets to all not only incurs the displeasure of the confidant who let it out to one and who disclosed it but it makes one defenceless against the onslaughts of others, for which they quote one's own words. This situation prepares a trap of self-strangulation like a snake getting chocked to death in its own cavity.]

आत्मवग परित्यत्य परवग समाश्रयेत्।
स्वयमेव लयं याति यथा राज्यमधर्मत: ।। 265 ।।

Aatmavargam Parittyajjya Parvargam Samaashret.
Svyaamev Layam Yaati Yathaa Raajyamdharmatah.

Those who leave their own category and seek support of the other category perish like a country resorting to immoral means.

[One should't forgo one's own faith or way of leading life because change in it means resorting to some way about which you have no idea. It is 'Adharm' for the upholder of the forlorn faith. And while treading a new path one is likely to commit grave mistake, which may lead one to the way of doom. Chanakya avers Srimadbhagwat Gita's dictate that one should never leave one's way of working or in other words, one's category or else one is doomed.

आप्तद्वेषाद्‌ भवेन्मृत्युः परद्वेषात्त्सतु धनक्षयः।
राजद्वेषाद्‌ भवेननाशे ब्रह्मद्वेषात्कुलक्षयः ।। 266 ।।

Aaptdveshaat Bhavenmrittyuh Padveshaattu Dhanshayah.
Raajdveshad Bhavennasho Brahmadveshaat Kulakshayah.

Enmity with the noble-men and Sadhus (hermits) causes one's death; with the adversary causes dissipation of wealth; with the king causes total ruin and with the brahman causes even cessation of one's lineage.

राज्ञेधर्मणि धर्मिष्ठाः पापे पापाः समे समाः।
राजानमनुवर्तन्ते यथा राजा तथा प्रजाः ।। 267 ।।

Raagye Dharmani Dharmishthaah Paape Paapaah Same Samaah.
Rajanamanuvartante Yathaa Raajaa tathaa Prajaa.

Subjects follow their king: they are heathen if the king be irreligious; sinners if the king be a sinner and normal if their king be normal. As the king so the subjects.

[The last phrase of this famous quotation is very well known. In the modern concept, it could be interpreted as the people follow their leaders.

> **पुस्तकेषु च या विद्या परहस्तेषु च यद्धनम्।**
> **उत्पन्नेषु च कार्येषु न सा विद्या न तद्धनम् ।। 268 ।।**

Pustakeshu Cha yaa Viddyahaa Parhasteshu Cha Yaddhanam.
Uttpanneshu Cha Kaaryeshu Na Saa Viddyaa Na Taddhanam.

The knowledge that remains confined to the books (and doesn't get retained in the reader's mind) and the money that has gone in other's hand; neither there is any use of that knowledge nor there is any worth of that money. The inference is obvious. Knowledge must have its application to enhance its value like money must be in one's control to be of any worth.

> **प्रियवाक्यप्रदानेन सर्वे तुष्यन्ति मानवा:।**
> **तस्मात् तदेव वक्तव्यं वचने का दरिद्रता ।। 269 ।।**

Priyavaakyapradaanen Sarve Tushyanti Maanavaah.
Tasmaat Tadev Vaktavyam Vachane Kaa Daridrataa.

Sweet language satisfies all. Hence all must be sweet in their language. Even the excessive use of sweet words does not render anyone poor.

> **कोहि भारत: समर्थानां किं दूरं व्यवसायिनाम्।**
> **को विदेश सुविद्यानां को पर: प्रियवादिनाम् ।। 270 ।।**

Kohi Bhaarah Samarthaanaam Kim dooram Vyavsaayinaam.

Ko Videsh Suviddyaanaam Koparah Priyavaadinaam.

Nothing is burdensome for a competent person. No place is far off for a trader, No land is a foreign strand for the scholar and no one is stranger for a man with a sweet tongue.

[A competent person knows how to solve his problem so nothing is burdensome for him. For the trader no place is far off if he can get the right price for his merchandise. The learned man or the scholar, by dint of his learning, knows how to get settle in any land. And, how can anybody be stranger for the person who has a sweet tongue? Sweet speech makes even the most diehard enemy, one's friend, let alone a stranger who bears no animus for anyone.]

तावन्मौने नीयन्ते कोकिलश्चैव वासराः।
यावत्सर्व जनानन्ददायिनी वाङ् न प्रवर्तते ।। 271।।

Taavannmaunem Neeyante Kokilashchaiv Vaasaraah.
Yaavatsarva Janaanandadaayinee Vaang Na Pravartate.

The koel keeps quiet till she is able to coo in its sweet voice. And her this cooing delights everybody.

[The koel coos up only during the spring. Otherwise, she keeps quiet. Then its cooing delights everybody's heart. Chanakya impliedly says that we must keep quite till we are able to converse only in a sweet voice.]

Learn which from what?

सिंहादेकं बकादेकं शिक्षेच्चत्वारि कुक्कुटात्।
वायसात्पंच शिक्षेच्च षट् शुनस्त्रीणि गर्दभात् ।। 272 ।।

Singhodekam Bakaadekam Sikshechattvaari Kukkutaat.
Vaaysaatpanch Shikshechshat Shat Shanstreeni Gardabhaat.

Learn one thing from the lion, one from heron, four from the cock, five from the crow, six from the dog and seven from the donkey. [Details ahead.]

य एतान् विंशतिगुणानाचरिष्यति मानवः।
कार्यावस्थासु सर्वासु अजय स भविष्यति ।। 273 ।।

Ya Etaan Vinshaatigunaanaacharishyati Manavah.
Karyaavasthaasu Sarvaasu Ajayh sa Bhavishyati.

If a man is able to adopt, at least, a score of teachings into his life, he shall ever be a successful person.

विनयं राजपुत्रोभ्यः पण्डितेभ्यः सुभाषितम्।
अनृतं धूतकारेभ्यः स्त्रीभ्यः शिक्षेत कैतवम् ।। 274 ।।

Vinayam Rajutrebhyah Panditephyah Subhashitam.
Anritam Dhyootakaarebhyah Streebhyah Shikshet Kaitavam.

Learn courtesy from the princes, sweet speech from the learned scholars, lying from the gamblers and deceit from the women.

[The princes are specially taught how to be courteous; how to carry themselves and how to behave, so they are the best source to learn about courtesy from; the learned knows where to use which word and with what effect to give more meaning to them. They are experts in conveying the most bitter meaning in the sweetest possible language. So, they are the best teacher to instruct in conversation. Owing to the demand of their profession the gamblers speak lies with such a flourish as to make them appear like the real truth: This art is to be learn from them. And, according to Chanakya, the women are past masters in the practice of deceit. They dupe so convincingly that many a wise man come a cropper against their hood winking expertise. So, the women are the best teacher in this field.]

From the Lion

प्रभूतं कार्यमपि वा तत्परः प्रकर्तुमिच्छति।
सर्वारम्भेण तत्कार्यं सिंहादेकं प्रचक्षते ।। 275 ।।

Prabhootam Kaaryamapi Vaa Tattparah Prakartumichati.
Sarvaarambhen Tattkaarya Singhaadekam Prachakshate.

Whether it be big or small, we must do every work with our full capacity and power. We must learn this quality from the lion.

[It is generally believed that the lion never does anything half heartedly. It would kill a rabbit or attack an elephant with its full ferocity. While acting this way we eliminate the possibility of suffering a set back out of the overconfidence of taking on our adversary.]

From the Heron

इन्द्रियाणि च संयम्य बकवत्पण्डितो नरः।
देशकाल बलं ज्ञात्वा सर्वकार्याणि साध्येत् ।। 276 ।।

Indrayaani Cha Sanyammya Bakavttyapandito Narah.
Deshkaal Balam Gyaattvaa Sarvakaaryaani Saadhayet.

Controlling all your senses like the heron, and after carefully considering the factors of time and space and the capacity of the self, the wise accomplish their work successfully.

[The heron has this great capacity to forget everythingelse to concentrate on its target: So, this capacity of concentrating one's mind on one's aim or target should be adopted by us in our life. With this level of consideration and the proper assessment of one's power vis-a-vis the time and place if the wise act, they are bound to succeed, for success depends upon the able assessment of one's situation, the power of concentration and the capacity to put in one's total might should the need arise.]

From the Cock

प्रत्युत्थानं च युद्धं च संविभागश्च बन्धुषु।
स्वयमाक्रभ्यं भेक्तं च शिच्चत्वारि कुक्कुटात् ।। 277 ।।

Prattyuthaanam Chayuddham Cha Samvibhaayashcha Bandhushu.
Svayamaakrabhya Bhoktam Cha Shikshechchattvari Kukkutaat.

The cock can teach us four things : get up at the right time, fight bitterly, make your brothers flee and usurp and devour their share also.

[Although apparently these appear quite immoral teachings in the present context also, what is taught here are the lessons in self-preservation against all odd, which is a natural instinct.]

From the Crow

गुढ मैथुनकारित्वं काले काले च संग्रहम्।
अप्रत्त्वचनमविश्वासं पंच शिक्षेच्च वायसात् ।। 278 ।।

Goodha mainthunkarittvam kale-kale cha sangraham.

Appramattvachanam vishvassam panch Shiksheechcha Vaasyat.

Stealthy copulation, collecting things and augmenting your resourcefulness from time to time; be alert and not beliveing anybody, making enough noise to make all gather round you–these five things are to be learnt from the crow.

[This again is an instruction in the self-preservation. One marvels at the minute observation of Chanakya as a bird-watcher.]

From the Dog

बशी स्वलपसन्तुष्टः सुनिद्रो लघुचेतनः।
स्वामिीमाक्तश्च शूरश्च षडेते श्वानतो गुणाः ।। 279 ।।

Baahavshee Svalpasantushtah Sunidro Laguchetanaa.
Swaamibhaktashcha Shoorashcha Shadete Shvaanato Gunaah.

Deriving satisfaction out of a little eating even in the famished condition; be alert despite being deep in slumber, faithfulness and bravery–these six qualities ought to be learnt from the dog.

[The dog has this unique capacity to derive satisfaction with whatever it manages to procure; for its eating despite its famished condition. It sleeps very soundly but, instantly wakes up hearing any sound. It is believed to be the most faithful animal. It is also a brave animal even against the fiercest odd. In saving its own or its master's life, its murderous streak is unmatched.]

From the Donkey

सुश्रान्तोपि वहेद् भारं शीतोष्णं न पश्यति।
सन्तुष्टश्चरतो नित्यं त्रीणि शिक्षेच्च गर्दभात् ।। 280 ।।

Sushraantoapi Vahed Bhaaram Sheetoshna Na Pashyanti.
Santushtashcharato Nittyam Treeni Shikshechacha Gardabhaat.

The capacity to carry the load despite being bone-tired, being undaunted by the vagaries of weather and getting satisfied in all the conditions–these three qualities are to be learnt from the donkey.

How to control Whom

लुब्धमर्थेन गृह्णीयात्स्तब्धमंजलिकर्मणा।
मूर्खश्छन्दानुरोधेन यथार्थवादेन पण्डितम् ।। 281 ।।

Lubhhdhamurthen Grihaveeyaattstabdhamanjalikarmanaa.
Moorkashchandaanurodhen Yathaarthvaaden Panditam.

Control greedy by money, the arrogant by submissiveness, the fool by preaching and the learned by telling him the reality.

[First two observations are quite clear. The one dealing with the fool needs an elaboration. A fool is he who dosen't know what knows. When he is preached, he realises his ignorance and this realisation makes him a little grateful to the preacher who can, then, mould him easily. Fourth : you just can't fool an intelligent and learned man by mincing words or telling half truths to confuse him. His sharpness and intelligence would also expose the falsehood. So, it is always better if one tells the truth before such persons. Since, they are wise enough, they would realise the helplessness in the situation and accept whatever you ask them to. Straight forward talk is the best way to control or convince a Pundit or a learned and an intelligent man.]

Miscellaneous

स्कृज्जल्पन्ति राजान: सकृज्जल्पन्ति पण्डिता: ।
सकृत्कन्या: प्रदीयन्ते त्रीण्येतानिक सकृत्सकृत् ।। 282 ।।

Sakrijjalpanti Raajanah Sakrijjalpanti Panditaah.
Sakrittkannyaah Pradeeyante Treennyetaani Sakrittsakrit.

The kings speak but once, so do the learned scholars. The daughter is gifted once. These three actions are performed just once.

[The kings rarely repeat their order. Here 'speak' means to give orders. The voice of authority has to be listened with rapt attention, hence the utterance of the orderonly once is enough. The scholars give their observation, their opinion or their considered view pointonly once. Since, they speak after weighing all pros and cons, they speak less and do not repeat their; opinion or alter it. And gifting one's daughter to a deserving groom takes place only once, which is still the practice prevalent in most of the traditional families in India.]

एकाकिना तपो द्वाभ्यां पठनं गायनं त्रिभि: ।
चतुर्भिगमन क्षेत्रां पचभिर्बहुभि रणम् ।। 283 ।।

Ekaakinaa Tapo Dvaabhyaam Pathanaam Gaayanam Tribhi.
Chaturbhigaman Kshetram Panchabhirbahubhi Ranam.

For chanting of Mantras (worships) just one, for studies two, for singing three, at the time of going out (on foot) four, for working in the field five and many persons are required in the war.

[Worship isobvious performed best when one is alone. In the studies one companion help, in exchanging the notes and discussing the problems for the better comprehension of the lesson. In singing, the requirement of three person is essential for the accompaniment's sake. If one sings, the other gives accompaniment on the rhythm instrument (tabla,etc.) and the third person for the maintenance of the desired notes on the taanpuras: When going out on foot, four persons are needed to watch the four directions for any possible mishap. In the field, one is needed to water the plants, the other to clear the field of the unwanted growth, third to guard it against any unwanted intrusion, four to sow the seed and fifth to arrange the soil and look after the general maintenance of the field. Obviously, in war many persons are required to fight.]

जन्ममृत्युर्नियत्येको भुनक्त्येक: शुभाशुभम्।
नरकेषु पतत्येक: एको याति परां गतिम् ।। 284 ।।

Janmamrittyurniyattyeko Bhunakkttyekha Shubhashubham.
Narakeshu Patattyekah Eko Yaati Paraam Gatim.

A man comes alone in the world, meets his end alone; alone he bears the consequences of his good or evil deeds, alone he suffers the tortures of the hell and alone he attains to the ultimate state.

[Despite a man being dubbedas a social being in all major activities of his life, he is all alone. This way he shares nothing with any body. Chanakya reminds us this bitter truth that in this transient world nothing is permanent, neither any companionship nor any association.]

श्लोकेन वा तदद्धेन तदर्द्धर्दर्धक्षरेण वा।
अवन्ध्यं दिवसं कुर्याद् दानायनकर्मभि ॥ 285 ॥

Skloken Vaa Taddardhen Taddardhaaddardhaksharen Vaa.
Avanndhyam Divasam Kuryaad Danaadhyan Karmabhi.

One should always think over any Shloka or half or part of it or even a letter of it. This way brooding over (the pithy), ancient saying, studying and giving elms one should utilise one's each day.

[Brooding over, reflecting on and studying the scriptures and the other wise sayings one should pass his day. This way not only his intelligence would be sharpened and analytical power would also get improve but he would also be away from the various devastating distractions. Thus passing his free time in studying for the self-benefit and giving elms for the other's benefit, one utilizes one's each day usefully.]

श्रुत्वा ध्म विजानाति श्रुत्वा त्यजति दुर्मतिम्।
श्रुत्वा ज्ञानमवाप्नोति श्रुत्वा मोक्षमवाप्नुयात् ॥ 286 ॥

Shruttva Dharman Vijaanaatishruttva Tyajati Durmatim.
Shruttvaa Gyaanamvaapnoti Shruttvaa Mokshamavaapnnyaat.

It is through hearing (the facts) that a man realises what is his real Dharma, and through hearing only that he gives up his ignorance (or stupidity). It is through hearing that he acquires knowledge and attain to the Moksha (final Liberation).

[Man learns about his Dharma, gives up his evil mindedness (Durbudhi) and attains his final liberation only by listening to the wise teachings of his seniors, his Gurus, and other great persons. Chanakya says that these concepts cannot be attained by intuitive wisdom, but one learns about them from the external sources. Impliedly, he means that we all must listen to these wise teachings with rapt attention.]

भ्रमन्सम्पूज्यते राजा भ्रमन्सम्पूज्यते द्विज:।
भ्रमन्सम्पूज्यते योगी स्त्री भ्रमती विनश्यति ॥ 287 ॥

Bhramannsampoojyate Raajaa Bhramannsampoojyate Dvijah.
Bhramannsampoojyate Yogi Stree Bhramati Vinashyatee.

A roving king, a roving brahman and a roving Yogi are adored but a roving woman is doomed.

[An efficient ruler is always on the move i.e. he is always gathering the first hand information to set his administration right. The subjects adore him for his ability to move about his State and solve their problems. A brahman lives in communion with eternity, hence he shouldn't be attached to any particular place or person, for him the whole world is in the manifestation of the divine spirit. Practical interpretation of this aphorism would be that the more movement a brahman does, the more knowledge he acquires and hence he wins others adoration. The same is true with the Yogi. But if a woman keeps on moving, she exposes her to a variety of dangers, each being potent enough, in our society set-up, to bring her to disrepute, or the way to doom.]

काल: पचति भूतानि काल: संहरते पजा:।
काल:सुप्तेशु जागर्ति कालो हि दुरतिक्रम: ॥ 288 ॥

Kaalah Pachati Bhootaani Kaalah Sanharte Prajaah.
Kaalah Suptesh Jaagarti Kaalo Hinduratikramah.

Time devours the beings and destroys the creation. It remains active even when the beings are asleep. No one can check its incessant flow.

[Time is all powerful and ever active. Its ruthless counting continues even if we may be asleep or not conscious. No one can check its flow. All are helpless before time.]

गन्धं सुवर्णे फलमिक्षुदण्डे
नाकारिपुष्पं खलु चन्दनस्य।
विद्वान ध्नीभूपतिदीर्घजीवी
धतुः पुरा कोऽपि न बुद्धिदोऽभूत ।। 289 ।।

Gandham Suvarne Phalmikshudande
Naakaaripushpam Kalu Chandanasya.
Viddvan Dhanee Bhoopatideerghajeevee
Dhaatuh Puraa kiapina Bhuddhidoabhoot.

Gold has no fragrance, sugarcanes have no fruits and the sandalwood has no flowers. A scholar is never wealthy and a king is never long aged. Why did this presciences was not given to Brahma (the creator).

[All good things are not perfect. The best metal gold satisfies all other senses but has no fragrance. Similarly, sugarcane, the best stem, is fruitless and the sandal, the best wood has no flower. Chanakya says, had the creator been advised earlier, he would have made these minor deficiencies correct in order to bring his creation perfect. Impliedly, it also means that nothing is perfect in the world.]

पिता रत्नाकरो यस्य लक्ष्मीर्यस्य सहोदरी।
शंखो भिक्षाटनं कुर्यात्र दत्तमुपतिष्ठिति ।। 290 ।।

Pitaa Rattnaakaro Yasya Laxamirasya Sahodari.
Shakho Bhikshaatanam Kuryaann Dattamupatishthati.

He whose father sea is the mine of the precious gems, whose real sister is the goddess (of wealth) Lakshmi, that conch-shell has to resort to begging. What could be more anomalous than this?

[Conchshells are also produced by the sea. It is believed in the Hindu Mythology that the Goddesss Lakshmi originated from the sea. This way she is a sister to the conch-shell as both are produced by the same father sea. Sea is also supposed to be the place of origin of many a gem. The conch shells are otherwise worthless, barring their use in creating a peculiar sound: So building his full allegory, Chanakya opines with a touch of irony that even with such rich relations, the conch-shell has to survive begging.]

सवौर्षधीनाममृतं प्रधनं।
सर्वेषु सौख्येष्वशनं प्रधनम्।
सर्वेन्द्रियाणां नयनं प्रधनं
सर्वेषु गात्रोषु शिरः प्रधनम् ।। 291 ।।

Sarvausheedheenaamamritam Pradhaanam
Sarveshu Saukhyaeshvashanam Praddaanam.
Sarveindriyaanaam Mayanm Pradhaanam
Sarveshu Gaatresu Shirah Pradhaanam.

Among all the herbal medicines, the chief is Amrit (Gilory & a vary efficacious medicinal creeper); among all the pleasures' the chief is partaking of food; among all the senses–sight (eyes) is the chief and among all the organs the chief is the head.]

समाने शोभते प्रती राज्ञि सेवाच शोभते।
वाणिज्य व्यवहारेषु स्त्री दिव्या शोभते गृहे ।। 292 ।।

Samaane Shobhate Pretee Raagyi Sevaa Cha Shobhate.
Vaanijjyam Vyavhaareshu Streedivyaa Shobate Grihe.

Friendship among the equals and service to the king look good. It is befitting for the Vaishya (trader-class) to be in business and for a noble lady to be in the house (i.e. a noble lady's presence makes the house look charming).

गुणे भूषयते रूपं शीलं भूषयते कुलम्।
सिद्धिर्भूषयते विद्यां भोगो भूषयते धनम् ।। 293।।

Guno Bhooshyate Roopam Sheelam Bhooshayate Kulam.
Siddhirbhooshayate Viddyaam Bhogo Bhooshayate Dhanam.

Virtues enhance the beauty of the form; good manners enhance the glory of the family; perfection enhances the value of education and enjoyment enhances the pleasures of wealth.

कोकिलानां स्वरो रूपं नारी रूपं पतिव्रतम।
विद्या रूपं कुरूपाणां क्षमा रूपं तपस्विनाम् ।। 294 ।।

Kokilaanam Svaro Roopam Naaree Roopam Pativratam.
Viddyaa Roopam Kshamaa Roopam Tapasvinaam.

The beauty of the koel lies in its voice; that of the woman in her wifely faithfulness to her husband. The beauty of the ugly lies in their learning and that of the ascetics in the forgiveness.

अध्वा जरं मनुष्याणां वाजिनां बन्धंजरा।
अमैथुनं जरा स्त्रीणां वस्त्राणामामातपं जरा ।। 295 ।।

Addhva Jaram Manushyaanaam Vijinaam Bandhanam Jaraa.
Amaithunam Jaraa Streenaam VAstraanaa Maatapam Jaraa.

Travel ages a man, immobility ages a horse; a woman ages when not copulated with and a clothe ages when dried in the sun.

मूर्खाणां पण्डिता द्वेष्या अधनानां महाधन।
वारांगना कुलीनानां सुभगानां च दुर्भगा ।। 296 ।।

Moorkahanaam Panditaa Dveshyaa Adhnaanaam Mahaadhanaa.
Vaaraanganaa Kuleenaanaam Subhagaanaam Cha Durbhagaa.

Fools nurse ill-will for the scholars, the pauper for the rich, the prostitutes for the noble-familybrides and the widows for the married woman with their husband alive.

आचार: कुलमाख्याति देशमाख्याति भाषणम।
सम्भ्रम: स्नेहमाख्यति वपुराख्याति भोजनम ।। 297 ।।

Aachaarah Kulamaakhyati Deshamaakhati Bhaashanaam.
Sambhramah Snehamaakahyaati Vapuraakhyaati Bhojanam.

Manners betray one's family, and the language one's country. Hospitality betrays one's love and the physique betrays one's food intake.

अभ्यासाद्धार्यते विद्या कुलं शीलेन धर्यते।
गुणेन ज्ञायते त्वार्य कोपो नेत्रोण गम्यते ।। 298 ।।

Abhyaasaaddhaaryate Viddyaa Kulam Sheelen Dhaaryate.
Gunen Gyaayate Tvaarya Kopo Netren Gammyate.

Practice reveals one's learning, demeanour the lingeage; the virtues reveal one's quality and the eyes one's anger.

विद्यार्थी सेवक: पान्थ: क्षुधर्तो भयकातर:।
भाण्डारी च प्रतिहारी सप्तसुप्तानप्रबोधयेत ।। 299 ।।

Viddhyaarthee Sevakah Panthah Khulhartho Bhayakaataraah.
Bhandaaree Cha Pratihaaree Saptasaptaan Prabhodhayet.

Wake the following seven up from the slumber (without any hitch): the student, servant, the traveler,the one stricken with hunger, the frightened person; the store incharge and the watchman.

[i.e. there is no harm to wake these persons up even from the deep slumber as it is to their own benefit that they should be awakened.]

अहि नृपं च शार्दूलं वराटं बालकं तथा।
परश्वानं च मूर्ख च सप्तसुप्तान्न बोधयेत् ।। 300 ।।

Ahim nripam Cha Shaardoolam Varaatam Baalakam Tathaa.
Parshvaanam Cha Moorkha Cha Saptasuptaann Bodhyatet.

Do not wake the following up: snake, the king, the wasp, a

child, other's dog and the fool. They are better left sleeping.

[They all becomes dangerous or disturbing when woken up from the deep slumber.]

इक्षुदण्डास्तिलारू शूद्रा कान्ताकाच्चनमेदिनी।
चंदन दधि ताम्बूलं मद्रनं गुणवर्धनम ।। 301।।

Ikshudandaastilaah Shoodraa Kaantaakaanchanmedinee.
Chandanam Dadhi Taamboolam ardanam Gunavardhanam.

Sugercane, sesamum seeds, menial worker of the low caste, wife, gold, earth, sandal wood, curd, betel leaf–the more they are rubbed the more their qualities improve.

[Rubbing here includes griding, crushing, exorting maximum service, beating and pressing hard, etc., these may he suitably applied with the above mentioned objects.]

दरिद्रता धीरतया विराजते
कुवस्त्राता स्व्छतया विराजते।
कदननता चोष्णतया विराजते
कुरुपता शीलतया विराजते ।। 302 ।।

Daridrataa Dheertayaa Virrajate
Kuvastrataa Svachatayaa Virrajate.
Kadannataa Choshnatayaa Viraajate
Kuruptaa Sheetaltayaa Virrajate.

Patience lends grace to even poverty; clean clothes haloes their quality; the stale food appears tempting when heated up and the good manners and behaviour hide even the ugliness.

वृथा वृष्टि समुद्रेषु वृथा तृप्तेषु भोजनम।
वृथा दानं ध्नाढयेषु वृथा दीपो दिवापि च ।। 303 ।।

Vrithaa Vrishtih Samudreshu Vrithaa Tripteshu Bhojanam.
Vrithaa Daanam Dhanaadhyeshu Vrithaa Deepo Divaapi Cha.

Rains over the sea are useless, so is feeding to the well fed, giving alms to a rich man and burning a lamp in the day time.

भस्मनाशुद्धयेत कास्यं ताम्रमम्लेन शुद्धयति।
राजसा शुद्धयेत नारी नदी वेगेन शुद्धयति ।। 304 ।।

Bhasmanaa Suddhyate Kaassaya Taamramammlen Shudhyati.
Raajasaa Suddhyate Nareree Nadee Vegen Suddhyatati.

Bronze gets cleansed with the ash, copper with an acid; a women gets cleaned by menstruation and the rivers by their speedy flow.

शुद्धं भूमिगतं तोयं शुद्धा नारी पतिव्रता।
शुचि क्षेमकरो राजा सन्तोषी ब्राह्मण शुचिः ।। 305 ।।

Shuddham Bhoomigatam Togam Shuddhaa Naaree Pativrataa.
Shuchi Sschemakaro Raajaa Santoshee Brahamana Shuchin.

The sub-teranean water, a faithful wife, the king looking after the welfare of his subjects devotedly and a content brahmans are always poius.

वाचा च मनसः शौचमिन्द्रियनिग्रहः।
सूर्वभूतदया शोचमेतच्छौचं परमार्थिनाम ।। 306 ।।

Vaacha Cha Mansaa Shauchmindriyanigrah.
Sarvabhootadaya Shauchmetachaucham Parmaarthinaam.

The greatest piety lies in keeping one's thoughts and speech pure in practising continuence, in showing mercy to all beings and in doing good to others.

अन्तर्गतमलो दुष्टस्तीर्यस्नानशतैरपि।
न शूद्ध यति तथा भाण्डं सुरया दहितं च तत् ।। 307 ।।

Antargamalo Dushtasteeryasnaanshatairapi.
Na Shudh Yati Tatha Bhaandam Suryaa Daahitam Chata.

Like the wine pot, which does not get purified even after burning it in the fire, so the malice from the heart of the wicked does not get remove even after repeated ablutions in the holy waters.

एकोदरसमुभ्द्भूता एक नक्षत्रा जातका।
न भवन्ति समा शीले यथा बदरिकण्टका: ।। 308 ।।

Ekodarsamuddhootaa Eknakshatru Jaatakaa.
Na Bhavanti Samaasheele Yathaa Badrikantakaah.

Even if the womb of the origin and the birth-constellation be the same, two persons may still differ in their temperament and demenour, like, for example, the plum and the thorn.

[The plum tree has the fruit and the thorns jutting out of the same branch. Despite their closeness they differ drastically.]

दोपो भक्षयते वान्तं कज्जलं च प्रसूयते।
यदन्नं भक्षयते नित्यं जायते तृाशी प्रजा ।। 309 ।।

Deepo Bhakshayate Dvaantam Kajjalam Cha Prasooyate.
Yaddannam Bhakshayate Nittyam Jaaye Taadrishee Prajaa.

The lamp the darkness and produces soot-power: It means one produces according to whatever one eats.

[Chanakya says that the nature and behaviour of the progeny is very much dependent upon the intake of the progenitor.]

अन्नाद दशगुणं पिष्टं पिष्टाद्‌ दशगुणं पयं।
पयसोऽष्ट गुणं मांसं मांसाद दशगुणं धृतगुणं धृतम्‌ ।। 310 ।।

Annaad Dashgunam Pishtam Pishtaad Dashgunam Payah.
Payasoashtam Gunam Maansam Maansaad Dashgunam Ghritam.

The flour gives ten times more strength than the ordinary cereal; milk gives ten times strength more than the flour; meat gives ten times more strength than milk but ghee gives ten time more strength than even the meat.

[According to Chankya, ghee (or clarified butter) gives maximum strength to its consumer.]

इक्षुराप: पयोमूलं ताम्बूलं पफलमौषधम।
भक्षयतित्वापि कर्तव्या स्नानादानादिका: क्रिया: ।। 311।।

Ikshuraapah Payaomoolam Taamboodam Phadamaushadham.

Bhakshayatittvaapi Kartavyaa Sanaandaanaadikaah Kriyaah.

Even after having sugarcane, water, milk, roots, betel-leaf, fruits and (the herbal) medicines, one can perform the acts of self-ablution and worship, etc.

[One can perform the holy acts of worship, etc., even after having these things specifically and not after having other things.]

अजीर्णे भेषजं वारिजर्णे तद् बलप्रदम्।
भोजने चामृतं वारि भोजनान्ते विषप्रदम् ।। 312 ।।

Ajeerne Bheshajam Vaari Jeerne Tadd Balpradam.
Bhojane chamritam Vasri Bhojanaante vishpradam.

In indigestion water acts like a medicine. After digestion water gives strength (when imbibed). Drinking water during the meals acts like a nectar but if drink immediately after meals it acts like a poison.

सन्तोषामृततृप्तानां यत्सुखं शान्तिरेव च।
न च तद्धनलुबधनमितश्चेतश्च धवताम् ।। 313 ।।

Santoshaamritriptaanaam Yatsukham Shaantirev Cha.
Nacha Taddhanlubdhaanaamitshchetashcha Dhaavataam.

The pleasure, which the persons content with the nectar of satisfaction, receive is inaccessible to those who hanker after money.

[According to Chanakya, satisfaction is achievable through one's bent of mind and not owing to any external factor. Whereas, those who hanker after money; never derive satisfaction, those with this bent achieve it easily.]

तृणं ब्रह्मविद् स्वग तृणं शूरस्य जीवनम्।
जिमाक्षस्य तृणं नारी नि:स्पृहस्य तृणं जगत् ॥ 314 ॥

Trinam Brahamavid Svargam Trinam Sooransya Jeevanam.
Jimaakshyassya Trinam Naree Nihspihassya Trinam Jagat.

The heavens to the knower of the supreme; life to a chivalrous warrior; woman to the continent man and the whole world to the desireless person appear as worthless as a straw.

जले तैलं खले गुह्यं पात्रो दानं मनागपि।
प्राज्ञे शास्त्रं स्वयं याति विस्तारे वस्तुशक्तित: ॥ 315 ॥

Jale Tailam Guhyam Paatre Danam Manaagapi.
Praagye Shaastram Svayam Yaati Vishtaare Vastushaktitah.

Oil (drop) on (the surface of) water; a secret leaked out to wicked person; help to the deserving and knowledge to the wise spread (and swell) automatically.

पुनर्वित्तं पुनर्मित्रां पुनर्भार्यां पुनर्मही।
एतत्सर्वं पुनर्लभ्यं न शरीरं पुन: पुन: ॥ 316 ॥

Punarvittam Punarmitram Punarbhaaryaa Punarmahee.
Etattsarvam Punarlabhyam Na Shareeram Punch Punah.

One may get money, friend, the (dwelling on the) earth again but not one's body.

[i.e., one can get everything again, in this world but not life.

Since life is represented through a body, this term is being used symbolically.]

दुरऽस्थोपि न द्वरस्थो यो यस्य मनसि स्थित।
यो यस्य ह्रदये नास्ति समीपसथोऽपिद्वरत: ।। 317 ।।

Doorasthoapi Nadoorasthoyo Yasya Manasi Sthitah.
Yoyassya Hridaya Naasti sameepasthoapi Dooratah.

He who is inside one's heart (figuratively) is not far away despite being distant. He who is not in one's heart is very far off despite being close.

[He whom we love, is never far away despite being distant and he, whom we don't love, is very far away even if he be nearby physically.]

पृथिव्यां त्रीणि रत्नानि अननमाप: सुभोषितम्।
मूढै: पाषाणखण्डेषु रत्नसंज्ञां विधीयते।। 318 ।।

Prithivvaam Treeni Rattnaani annamaapah Subhoshitam Moodhai Paashaankhandeshu Ratnasangyaa Vidheeyate.

The real gems on this earth are three: food, water and kind words. Fools in vain call the pieces of stone as gems.

[Food, drink and kind words are the most precious things on the earth which gratify the basic physical and emotional needs.]

संद्य: प्रज्ञां हरेत्तुण्डो सद्य: प्रज्ञा करो वचा।
सद्य: शक्तिहरा नारी सद्यं: शक्तकरं पय: ।। 319 ।।

Saddyaapraggyaam Haretundo Saddyah Praggyaa Karo Vachaa.

Saddhyah Shaktiharaa Naaree Saddyah Shaktakara Payah.

Tunda (kundaroo) herb quickly destroys the intelligence, but vacha (a herb) revives it. Woman quickly depletes a man's potency but milk immediately restores it.

[Ayurveda also believes it that if a man drinks hot milk quickly after copulation, his strength gets revived.]

शाकेन रोगा: वर्धन्ते पयसा वर्धते तनु:।
धृतेनवर्धते वीर्य मांसान्मांसं प्रववर्धते ॥ 320 ॥

Shoken Rogaah Vardhante Payasaa Vardhate Tanuh.
Ghriten Vardha'e Veeryam Maansaanmaansam Pravardhate.

Sorrow aggravates diseases; milk nourishes body quickly; ghee enhances semen in the body and meat-eating only adds to the flesh of the body.

एक वृक्षे समारूढा नानावर्णविहंगमा:।
प्रभाते दिक्षु गच्छतिन्त तंत्रा का परिवेदना ॥ 321 ॥

Ekvrikshe Samaaroodhaa Naanaavarnavihangamaah.
Prabhaae Dikshu Gaachahathi Tara Ka Parvedanaa.

Many hued birds, seated on a tree, leave for different directions in the morning. What is there to grieve about?

[All get separated in the world after meeting each other. Thus separation is the regular feature of the world. Why should this cause any grief?]

गीर्वाणवाणीषु विशिष्टबुद्धि।
स्तथाऽपिभाषान्तर लोलुपोऽहमृ।।
यथा सुरगणष्वमृते च सेविते
स्वर्गागनानामधृासवे रूचि: ।। 322 ।।

Geervaanvaaaneeshu Vishishtabudhi
Stathaapi Bhaashaantar Lolupoahamri.
Yathaa Surganeshvamrite Cha Sevite
Svargaaganaanaamdharaasave Ruchih.

Despite my being versed in the Sanskrit language I want to learn other languages just as the gods, despite having nectar available, hanker for imbibing the juice of the Apsaras (divine dancers) lips.

अध: पश्यसि किं बाले पतितं तव किं भूवि।
रे रे मूर्ख न जानासि गतं तारूण्यमौक्तिकम ।। 323 ।।

Adhah Pasyasi Kim Baale Patitam Tav Kim Bhuvi.
Rere Moorkha Na Jaanaasi Gatam Taarunnyamauktikam.

"Dame! what are you looking down for, on the ground?"'Fool! Don't you know that I have lost the pearl of my youthfulness.

[A comely girl bowed down her head, out of shyness, when she found a contumelious man gazing at her. The man asked: "What are you searching for, on the ground?" She replied, "Fool! I have lost the essence of my youthfulness."]

शैले शैले न मणिक्यं मौक्तिकं न गजे गजे।
साधवो नहीं सव्रत्रा चन्दनं न हि वने वने ।। 324 ।।

Shaile Shaile Manikyam Mauktikam Na Gajegaje.
Saadhavo Maheem Sarvatra Chandanam Na Hi Vavevane.

Every mountain does not have the gems nor every elephant's head the pearl. Neither noble man are found everywhere nor sandalwood in every forest.

[The pearl found in an elephant's head was believed to be the pearl of the best quality in the ancient times.]

मुखं धन्यं तदेवास्ति वदति मधुरं सदा।
क्लेशम हरति दीनानां वचनैः रसपूरितैः ।। 325 ।।

Mukham Dhannyam Tadevaasti VAdati Maduram Sadaa.
Klesham Harati Deenaanaam Vachanai Rasapooritai.

Blessed is the mouth that utters sweet speech and by its kind and affectionate sentence (words) destroy the distress of the poor.

[Meaning the sweet speech and kind words evanesce even the afflicted person's distress.]

नेत्रोते एव धन्ये ये अन्धनां मार्गदर्शकि।
रक्षतः कण्टकाकीर्णत मार्गातान विषमात्तथा ।। 326 ।।

Netrete Eva Dhannye Ye Andhaanaam Maorgadarshake.
Rakshatah Kantakaakeerhaat Maargaattan Vishmaattathaa.

Blessed are those eyes that guide the way of the blind and protect them from their straying on the thorn-ridden path. [The moral: the 'haves' must help the 'have-nots'.]

हस्तौ धन्यो परेषां यौ आधतान् हरत: सदा।
आश्रयौ यौ जनानां स्त: पतितानामितभूतले ।। 327 ।।

Hastah Dhannye Ye Andhaanaam Maorgadarshake.
Rakshatah Kantakaakeerhaat Maargaattan Vishmaattathaa.

Blessed are the hands that lend support to the helpless persons and help in solving their troubles.

कर्णौ धन्यौ शुभं वाक्यं यावाकण्यत: सदा।
सज्जनानां च संगत्या पिबत: वचनामृतम ।। 328 ।।

Karnau Dhannyau Shubham Vaakyam Yaavaakarhayatah Sadaa.
Sajjanaanaam Cha sangattyaa Pibatah Vachanaamritam.

Blessed are those ears that covet to hear the noble and auspicious speech and all the time imbibe the nectar of gentleman's voice.

पादौ धन्ये शुभे मार्गे चलत: चौ निरंतरम्।
कल्याणाय च जीवनां उद्यतौभवत: सदा।। ।। 329 ।।

Paadau Dhannye Shubhe Maarge Chalatah Chau Nirantaram.
Kalyaanaaya Cha Jeevaanaam Uddyataubhavatah sadaa.

Blessed are the feet ever eager to move on the path leading to everyone's welfare.

यथा वृक्षा फलन्तयत्रा परेषामुपकारकाः।
नरः तथैव स धन्यः परेभ्य यस्यजीवनमः ।। 330 ।।

Yathaa Vriksha Phalantyatra Pareshaamupakaarakaah.
Marah Tathaiv Sa Bhannyah Yasya Jeevanam.

Like the trees growing their fruits for others' benefit, blessed are those men who devote their life to the others' cause.

Sutras of Chanakya

1. सुखस्य मूलं धर्मः।

Righteous conduct is the root of happiness. The state and its ruler must know their Dharma (proper duty) since all its functions bring happiness when done according to proper knowledge of Dharma.

2. धर्मस्य मूलमर्थः।

The root of Dharma is finance. A good financial health ensures proper discharge of the duties in a state.

3. अर्थस्य मूलं राज्यम्।

The state's welfare is rooted in good finance.

4. राज्यमूलमिन्द्रियजमः।

Control over the senses – the feedback from people – is the root of a state's welfare. The state should formulate its policies according to the feedback it receives from the people with proper modification.

5. इंद्रियजयस्य मूलं विनयः।

Humility is the root of the control of senses of a state. When the state authorities deal with people with humility they get proper and right response from the people.

6. विनयस्य मूलं वृद्धोपसेवा।

The root of humility is in the service of the seniors – elderly or old persons. When one renders honest service to elders one learns the worth of humility.

7. वृद्धसेवया विज्ञानत्।

By serving the old people (or elders) one gets the true knowledge.

8. विज्ञानेनात्मानं सम्पादयेत्।

True knowledge helps the king (or authority) discharge his duties more efficiently.

9. सम्पादितात्मा जितात्मा भवति।

The king who knows his functions or duties well can rule better because he can control his activities judiciously. Hence he gets all prosperity.

10. जितात्मा सर्वार्थे सं युज्येत।

He who controls his senses has his all wishes fulfilled. He gets wealth and prosperity in every way.

11. अर्थसम्पत् प्रकृति सम्पदं करोति।

Prosperity of the king (the ruling authority) ensures prosperity of people, for if man is prosperous, nature also helps in his prosperity.

12. प्रकृति सम्पदा ह्यनायकमति राज्यं नीयते।

Even a rulerless kingdom works well if its people are prosperous. [That is, if even a state has no ruler, people if prosperous, can supplement this deficiency by their financial capabilities.]

13. प्रकृतिकोप: सर्वकोपेभ्यो गरीयान।

The wrath of the Nature is the worst wrath.

14. अविनीतस्वामिलाभाद्द स्वामिजाय: श्रेयान्।

It is better to have no king than a king who doesn't know humility. [An inconsiderate king is worse than having no king.]

15. सम्पद्यात्मानविच्छेत् सहायवान।

An able king can train his assistant into efficiency and then he can rule efficiently. [If the king is able he can get a team of his capable assistants and then he can rule well.]

16. नासहायस्य मन्त्रनिश्चयः।

Without good assistants a king can take no right decisions. [Meaning the king must be assisted by good assistants if he wants to take right decisions.]

17. नैकं चक्रं परिभ्रमयति।

A single wheel can't move the chariot. [Indirectly, Chanakya says that alone a king can't function well. He must get the support of his able cabinet. The king and his cabinet are the two wheels of the state-chariot.]

18. सहायः सम सुखदुःख।

The assistant (or minister to a king) must help the master evenly in the latter's weal and woe. [The assistant shouldn't desert the master in latter's misery.]

19. मानी प्रतिमानीनमात्मनि द्वितीयं मन्त्रमुत्पादयेत्।

A thoughtful king must weigh pros and cons of a complex problem's solution within mind before reacting his final decision.

20. अविनीतं स्नेहमात्रेण न मन्त्रे कुर्वीत।

Never make a head-strong person your close confidant no matter how dear he / she may be to you. [A head-strong person can be provoked to spill out even the closely guarded secrets. Hence however dear he / she be, that person doesn't deserve to be made a confidant by the king.]

21. श्रुतवन्तमुपधाशुद्धं मन्त्रिणं कुर्वीत।

A king should choose only a well-learned and of strong character person as his minister. A minister should have an open mind and unflinchable loyalty to his king.

22. मन्त्रमूला: सर्वारम्भा: ।

Before starting any project (by the king), long deliberations are indispensable.

23. मन्त्ररक्षणे कार्यसिद्धिर्भवति।

Success in the project is achieved only when the prior deliberations are held as closely guarded secrets.

24. मन्त्रविस्त्रावी कार्य नाशयति।

Leakage of the state's secrets will destroy the projects.

25. प्रमादाद द्विषितां वशमुपपास्यति।

Callousness gets your secrets revealed to your enemy. [Hence the state must guard its secrets securely.]

26. सर्वद्वारेभ्यो मन्त्रो रक्षयितव्यः।

State secrets must be guarded against any possible leakage. [Don't let your state secrets be passed through any opening. Keep them closely guarded.]

27. मन्त्रसम्पदा राज्यं वर्धते।

Protection of the state's secrets ensures its continuous prosperity.

28. (a) श्रेष्ठतमां मन्त्रगुप्तिमाहुः।

It is best to keep the state's secret always closely guarded.

(b) कार्यन्धस्य प्रदीपो मन्त्रः।

Like in darkness the lamp shows the way, so in state administration when the king may feel darkness of confusion, his guide will always be wise deliberations (with his ministers).

29. मन्त्रचक्षुषा परछिद्राण्व लोकयन्तिः।

The king gets the eyes-through deliberations with his cabinet to get a peep into his enemy's weaknesses.

30. मन्त्रकाले न मत्सरः कर्तव्यः।

While deliberating upon the state affairs the king must not underestimate his cabinet's advice or show adamance in forcing his views.

31. त्रयाणामेकवाक्ये सम्प्रत्ययः।

When the three sides [that of the king's view, the advisor's opinion and the minister's suggestion] concur on one decision, the deliberations will surely be crowned with success in any state endeavour.

32. कार्यकार्यतत्त्वार्थदर्शिनो मन्त्रिणः।

A minister is an able minister only if he can shift clearly through what needs to be done and what not.

33. षट्कर्णाद् भिद्यते मन्त्रः।

A secret gets leaked if it falls into six ears. [The state secret must remain with only two persons: the king and the concerned minister. For if a third person – no matter how close – knows about it, it would be out in the open.]

34. आपत्सु स्नेहसंयुक्तं मित्रम्।

A friend is a true friend if he maintains affectionate relations even during the period of your distress. [A friend in need is friend indeed.]

35. मित्रसंग्रहेण बलं सम्पद्यते।

A group of friends makes one powerful. [A true friend is defined in the preceding sutra. Such friends group indeed makes one powerful.]

36. बलवान् अलब्धलाभें प्रयतते।

A powerful king or man tries to seek the impossible. Only a powerful king can afford to be audacious. Only then he tries to achieve something inaccessible so as to add to his strength and glory.

37. अलब्धलाभो नालस्य।

The lazy can't get any impossible gain. [Since the lazy do not make any effort, it is impossible for them to get any inaccessible advantage.]

38. आलस्य लब्धमपि रक्षितं न शक्यते।

The lazy can't protect even the advantage already received.

39. न आलसस्य रक्षितं विवर्धतेः।

The lazy owing too their lack of efforts can't ensure the growth of their assets.

40. न भृत्यान् प्रेषयति।

Lazy kings do not even make their sevants work.

41. अलब्धलाभादिचतुष्टयं राज्यतन्त्रम्।

It is essential for a state to ensure four inaccessible gains: to get what it doesn't have; to ensure its security after it is gained; to ensure growth in that asset thus gained; and to swap that gain with something more advantageous to the state.

42. राज्यतन्त्रायत्तं नीतिशास्त्रम्।

The structure to formulate policy for the state should always be the part of the stateadministration.

43. राज्यतन्त्रेष्वायत्तौ तन्त्रवापौ:।

The structure for formulating the home-policy and foreign policy must be an intrinsic part of the state-administration.

44. तन्त्र स्वविषयकृत्येष्वायत्तम्।

Home policy must relate to the interior matters of the state.

45. अवापो मण्डलनिविष्ट:।

Foreign policy relates to dealing with foreign countries.

46. संधिविग्रहयोनिर्मण्डल: ।

Pacts and agreements/treaties with other countries is an endless affair. [The king must be aware of his pacts/treaties with foreign countries all the time. Only then can be derived advantage from them at the suitable time.]

47. नीति शास्त्रानुगो राजा: ।

The king's competence is judged by not only his formulating apt policies but by also following them sincerely. [The king must not waiver from the policy he has once formulated. For this may tempt his ministers etc. to follow him and thus indiscipline will be bred in the stateadministration.]

48. अनन्तरप्रकृति: शत्रु: ।

The countries at the border with which we have frequent skirmishes eventually turn our enemies.

49. एकान्तरितं मित्रमिष्यते।

Enemy's enemy becomes our friend. [A common enemy makes even the hostile countries turn friends.]

50. हेतुत: शत्रुमित्रे भविष्यत: ।

One gets friends or enemies owing to some reason. [Friendship and enmity cannot emerge without any inherent reason.]

51. हीयमान: सधिं कुर्वीत।

The weak must not delay in having a peace-treaty with the powerful.

52. तेजो हि सन्धानहेतुस्तदर्थानाम्।

The personal strength of two peace makers is the binding cause of a treaty. [When two countries have matching strength and influence, their treaty is a really long lasting treaty.]

53. नातप्तलौहो लौहेन सन्धीयते।

If a piece of iron is not hot, it won't join with other iron piece. [Two countries of matchingstrength can be bound by a long lasting treaty.]

54. बलवान हीनेन विग्रणीयात्।

The powerful should always attack the less powerful. [It is an obvious strategy. Any attack on thepowerful will get you generally an adverse consequence.]

55. न ज्यायसा समेन वा।

Never attack someone more powerful or even of matching strength. [One should be cautious ofassessing one's strength before starting an aggression. Keep postponing any armed conflict till one is ensured of an edge over one's adversary.]

56. गजपादयुद्धमिव बलवद्विग्रहः।

Fighting against more powerful enemy is like foot soldiers taking on the elephant brigade. It would be just a suicidal endeavour!

57. आमपात्रमामेन सह विनश्यति।

Collision of the two receptacle made of the raw earth results in fragmentation of both. [If two adversaries of immature strength fight with each other, both shall perish.]

58. अरिप्रयत्नमभिसमीक्षेत्।

Always keep on assessing the enemy's endeavour. [One should always update oneself of one's enemies activities through secret intelligence and other means. Never take enemy's strength for granted.]

59. सान्धायैकतो वा।

Even if you have a treaty or pact with the neighbouring country, still keep on knowing about its activities through constant surveillance.

60. अमित्रविरोधात्मरक्षामावसेत्।

Always monitor the activities of the enemy's sleuths.

61. शक्तिहीनो बलवन्तमाश्रयेत्।

A powerless (or less powerful) king should seek the shelter of a powerful king.

62. दुर्बलाश्रयो दुःखमावहति।

Granting shelter to the weak gives much trouble and pain.

63. अग्निवद्राजानमाश्रयेत्।

Seek a king's shelter with abundant caution like one seeks the shelter of fire. [Fire may burn if you are not cautious and the king may punish if you are careless.]

64. राज्ञः प्रतिक्लं नाचरेत्।

Your behaviour should run counter to the king's orders.

65. उद्धतवेषधारो न भवति!

One must never be uncouthly dressed. [No matter what one's position be, one's dress must not appear to be an eye-sore to the observer.]

66. न देवचरितं चरेत्।

One must not copy king's manners or his life style. [No matter how much money and pelf you may acquire, your wearing a crown will appear bodacious since it is king's prerogative. A king has his royal style which a commoner shouldn't adopt to.]

67. द्वयोरपीर्ष्यतोद्वधीभावं कुर्वीत्।

Always sow a seed of dissension between the persons nursing jealousy for you. [This Sutra also highlights the strategy of common sense.]

68. नव्यसनपरस्य कार्यावाप्तिः।

A person addicted to some drugs or vile habits can never progress no matter what he or she does. [Their addiction will prevent them from paying attention to the job they undertake.]

69. इन्द्रियवशवर्ती चतुरंगवानपि विनश्यति।

If a king is slave to his senses, he shall perish even if he commands a well-endowed army. [Any sensual weakness may nullify whatever advantage his strong army may gain for a king.]

70. नास्ति कार्य द्यूतप्रवर्तस्य।

Anyone addicted to gambling can never complete any of his or her project.

71. मृगयापरस्य धर्मार्थ विनश्यत: ।

Those addicted to gambling lose their religious faith and wealth invariably. [Addiction is such a compelling obsession that one may transgress one's religious dictates and lose money in order to win one's stake.]

72. अर्थेषणा न व्यसनेषु गण्यते।

Longing for amassing wealth is not an addiction. [Since it could be deserve of nearly all. All want to be rich!]

73. न कामासक्तस्य कार्यनुष्ठानम्।

A lecherous person is good for nothing.

74. अग्निदाहादपि विशिष्टं वाक्पारुष्यम्।

Harsh language scalds more than the fire-burn! [For the wound or injury caused by fire could be healed but not the wound caused by a caustic remark.]

75. दण्डपारुष्यात् सर्वजनद्वेष्यो भवति।

A culprit should be punished by the judge according to the intensity of the crime committed by him and not out of any personal grudge. Such a judge will face the wrath of the people.

76. अर्थतोषिणं श्रीः परित्यजति।

A king who is satisfied with his wealth has opulence and riches soon deserting him. [Though true with all, the statement is specially true for the kings. Kings are always in need of money for ensuring welfare and development of his kingdom. How can a king be satisfied with his wealth? The moment he gets complacent in his endeavours, the high demands on the exchequer would deplete his coffers signifying the exit of opulence.]

77. अमित्रे दण्डनीत्यामायत्तः।

The existence of enemy depends on the policy of punishment. [The sterner be the policy of punishment, the lesser will be enemies. The converse is also true.]

78. दण्डनीतिमधितिष्ठन् प्रजाः संरक्षति।

A state protects its people by the judicious enforcement of the policy of punishment.

79. दण्डसम्पदा योजयति।

Proper punishment policy fills the royal coffers. [Proper punishment policy's enforcement will ensure better administration and law and order situation, thus consequently

80. दण्डाभावे मन्त्रिवर्गाभावः।

Absence of a proper punishment policy or penal code cause dearth of (good) Ministers in the state. [When the high positioned persons in a state have no fear of the penal code, they start indulging in reckless corrupt practices and not many are left in the cabinet to check them.]

81. न दण्डादकार्याणि कुर्वन्ति।

Lack of proper penal code enhance unlawful activities in the state. [It is an obvious condition. When people have no fear of punishment they may indulge in unlawful activities with vengeance.]

82. दण्डनीत्यामायत्तमात्मरक्षणम्।

Self-security (of the people) very much depends on the punishment policy in the state. [The sterner the policy the lesser will be the need for the self-security. Its converse is also true.]

83. आत्मनि रक्षिते सर्वं रक्षितं भवति।

Proper self-defence ensures everybody's self security. [If the king is well guarded, its subjects will also be well guarded. Thus everyone will have proper security and all will be safe.]

84. आत्मायत्तौ वृद्धिविनाशौ।

Growth and decay is always in one's own hands. [It is an obvious statement. Nobody can ensure any body's growth if that person is destroying oneself. And if one is determined to grow nobody can cause that person's destruction.]

85. दण्डो हि विज्ञाने प्रणीयते।

The penal code (in the state) must be enforced with discretionary wisdom. [The state cannot blindly enforce the penal code. While punishing the criminal that person's basic nature and past conduct must also be judged judiciously.]

86. दुर्बलोऽपि राजा नावमन्तव्यः।

Never dishonour even a weak king. [A king is not just a person but an institution for the state. Even if your king is weak he deserves honour because he symbolizes your state. Deshonouring him is tentamount to dishonouring your own country.]

87. नास्त्यग्नेर्दौर्बल्यम्।

Fire is never weak. [Even a tiny cinder can burn to ashes a huge jungle. Hence never disregard fire as weak any time.]

88. दण्डे प्रतीयते वृत्तिः।

One's punishment policy (or a king's penal code) reveals one's (king's) own basic nature. [A cruel-minded king will have a ruthless penal code which a soft-hearted king will have a lenient punishment policy. Thus the punishment policy will also reveal the king's basic nature.]

89. वृत्तिमूलमर्थलाभः।

Gain is the basic aim of any endeavour. [All work to gain some kind of benefit which is the aim of every profession as well.]

90. अर्थमूलौ धर्मकामौ।

The root of Dharma (religious belief) and Kama (satiation of desires) is Artha (some positive gain). [Note: Normally Artha in Sanskrit means meaning or purpose but Chanakya's view was the Artha meant gain of any kind and not only financial gain. That is why his famous treatise on the Statecraft is titled 'Arthashastra', for Chanakya believed that every activity of a state should be aimed to get benefit for the kingdom – be it social, financial and even spiritual. In this Sutra's context also, spiritual gain is the root of all religious practices and gain of physical satisfaction is the root of all desires.]

91. अर्थमूलं कार्यम्।

Money is the base of all the assignments.

92. यदल्पप्रयत्नात् कार्यसिद्धिर्भवति।

With that gain (refer to the previous sutra) even with the less efforts one achieves one's objective.

93. उपायपूर्वं न दुस्करं स्यात्।

If one has dedication to find a clue to solve a problem, no problem remains difficult. [One must have dedication and determination to solve any problem. Then no problem will remain insolveable.]

94. अनुपायपूर्वं कार्यं कृतमपिविनश्यति।

If one attempts to solve a problem without any determination and dedication even what is achieved in the process also gets destroyed (or wasted).

95. कार्यार्थिनामुपाय एव सहायः।

For the industrious finding a clue to solution of a problem is a great help.

96. कार्यं पुरुषकारेण लक्ष्यं सम्पद्यते।

A work is completed if one is determined to do it. Then it becomes one's sole aim.

97. पुरुषकारमनुवर्तते दैवम्।

Fortune favours the brave. [If one is determined to do a job, his fate follows him. That is, one gets support from even the divines agencies.]

98. दैवं बिनाऽति प्रयत्नं करोति यत्तद्विपफलम्।

God helps those who help themselves!

99. असमाहितस्य वृतिर्न विद्यते।

Fatalists get no job. [Those who wait for their luck to help them never get any work or employment to earn their livelihood.]

100.पूर्व निश्चित्य पश्चात् कार्यमारभेत।

Before starting any job, weigh all the possible pros and cons and then decide your course of action.

101. कार्यान्तरे दीर्घसूत्रता न कर्तव्या।

Be not slack before the whole job is finished. [Lazing mid-way a work, one may not finish it well or timely.]

102. न चलचित्तस्य कार्यावाप्तिः।

A fickle mind can never complete a job successfully.

103. हस्तगतावमानात् कार्यव्यतिक्रमो भवति।

Not using the available means properly interferes in

completing the work.

104. दोषवर्जितानि कार्याणि दुर्लभानि।

Doing a work flawlessly is a rare happening.

105. दुरनुबन्ध कार्य नारभेत्।

One must not take up the job whose consequence is not ascertained before hand.

106. कालवित् कार्य साध्येत्।

He who discerns the right time of doing a work gets sure success. [Every job has its specified or most opportune time to complete it. He who knows this invariably achieves success in doing it.]

107. कालातिक्रमात् काल एव फलं पिवति।

Interference in the flow of time eventually makes the time nullify its results. [In any work, an order of time should be maintained. If done haphazardly, the lapsing time may nullify its result.]

108. क्षण प्रति कालविक्षेपं न कुर्यात्सर्व कृत्येषु।

In no work, even a moment should be wasted. [In doing a work, not even a moment should be overlapped. If you lose a moment in the beginning, you can't replace with the extra moment in the end.]

109. देशफलविभागौ ज्ञात्वा कार्यमारभेत्।

Before doing a work its place and time must be found out. [Each work has its significance according to the place and time it is performed in. At one place or time it may be good while it may be harmful if done at other place and in a different time.]

110. दैवहीनं कार्यं सुसाध्यमपि दु:साध्यं भवति।

An easy work becomes difficult for the unlucky person!

111. नीतिज्ञो देशकालौ परीक्षेत्।

The wise must examine the contemporary situation of a country [before making their decision].

112. परीक्ष्यकारणी श्रीश्चिरं तिष्ठति।

When begun after testing the consequence of a work, its results stay for long time with the performer. [He (or the king) who judges before hand the consequence of a campaign after testing its efficacy with respect to time and territory enjoys its results (or fruit) for a longer duration.]

113. सर्वाश्च सम्पत: सर्वोपायेन परिग्रहेत्।

All assets (wealth or riches) must be collected with all possible means. [A king who has to ensure welfare of his kingdom, must gather all sorts of resources with whatever means available, for he doesn't know which may come handy at what time.]

114. भाग्यवन्तमपरीक्ष्यकारिणं श्रीः परित्यजतिः।

Goddess of riches and resources, Lakshmi, parts company even with the lucky person who works without thinking beforehand the consequence of that work.

115. ज्ञानानुमानैश्च परीक्षा कर्तव्या।

Knowledge and guess, both, must be used while examining the possible consequence of a job to be undertaken.

116. यो यस्मिन् कर्मणि कुशलस्तं तस्मिन्नैव योजयेत्।

The job must be assigned on the basis of the expertise of its plausible performers.

117. दुःसाध्यमपि सुसाध्यं करोत्युपायज्ञः।

He who knows the tricks of the trade makes even the difficult job easy.

118. अज्ञनिना कृतमपि न बहु मन्तव्यम्।

Any job accomplished by the ignorants (accidentally) must not be given any importance.

119. यादृच्छिकत्वात् कृमिरपि रूपान्तराणि करोति।

[The Sutra should be read in continuation of the previous one.] For even the woodworms can form various designs penetrating the wood accidentally, they can't be held to be the artists at all. It is just by coincidence. The same way an ignorant fool can create something noteworthy but they shouldn't be given any importance.

120. सिद्धस्यैव कार्यस्य यप्रकाशन कर्तव्यम्।

One must publicise only that work which is complete and successful. [Publicizing an incomplete
job could tempt the opponents hurdle it mid-way].

121. शानवतामिप दैवमानुषदोषात् कार्याणि दुष्यन्ति।

The achievements of the knowledgeable or wise persons can also get sullied by the interference of fate or men.

122. दैवं शान्तिकर्मणा प्रतिर्षद्धव्यम्।

One must face the natural calamities with a calm head (and not in panic or desperation). [The adverse acts of providence or the natural calamities – like earthquakes, floods, drought, Tsunami etc. – invariably create panic and desperation in the mind of the human sufferer which further aggravate the bad situation. One should try to be calm which dealing with such a situation.]

123. मानवीं कार्यविपत्ति कौशलेन विनिवारयेत्।

The difficulties in work borne by men should be solved with wisdom.

124. कार्यविपत्तौ दोषान् वर्णयन्ति बलिशा: ।

It is only fools who start the blaming game when they face any problem in their work. [Instead, they should try to root out the cause of the problem. But fools do exactly opposite. They start blaming each other which may further compound the trouble.]

125. कार्यार्थिना दाक्षिण्यं न कर्तव्यम्।

Don't be kind towards the harmful persons (involved in a job). [One should be a hard-taskmaster to the person not doing their job properly.]

126. क्षीरार्थी वत्सो मातुरुध: प्रतिहन्ति।

Even a calf attacks on the udder of the mother cow when it wants milk. [The body-demands can even subdue the affection.]

127. अप्रयत्नात् कार्यविपतिर्भवति।

Lack of sincerity in efforts goes to ruin the work [in hand].

128. न दैवप्रमाणानां कार्यसिद्धिः।

The one who depends on luck never achieves success in his/ her assignments.

129. कार्यबाह्यो न पोषयत्याश्रितान्।

Those who run away from their responsibilities are never able to nurture their dependents properly.

130. यः कार्यं न पश्यति सोऽन्धः।

He who doesn't see his work is verilly a blind person. [One must properly analyse all the aspects before starting a job. He who doesn't do so is blind.]

131. प्रत्यक्षपरोक्षानुमानैः कार्याणि परीक्षेत्।

One must examine the work and the ways of doing it with the help of directly or indirectly available methods and means while judiciously supplementing them with his thoughtful estimations.

132. अपरीक्ष्यकारिणं श्री परित्यजति।

[In continuation with the previous Sutra] For those who work without such thinking are always deprived by success and its additional gains.

133. परीक्ष्य तार्या विपत्तिः।

When one finds problem arising in the work, one should examine all the aspects of it minutely to find the fault and remove it.

134. स्वशक्तिं ज्ञात्वा कार्यमारंभेत्।

Start any work after assessing totally your capability for doing it

135. स्वजनं तर्पयित्वा यः शेषभोजी सोऽमृतभोजी।

He who feeds his close ones before feeding himself verilly partakes of ambrosia. [One must fulfill the needs of his close ones – friends, dependents and guests etc. – before fulfilling his own. Then he will be the most satisfied person.]

136. सर्वानुष्ठानादायमुखानि वर्धन्ते।

One must not leave any possibility of enhancing one's resources/income. This will ensure his constant growth.

137. नास्ति भीरोः कार्यचिन्ता।

The cowards don't care for their work or duties. [A coward is actually a work-shirker].

138. स्वामिन: शीलं ज्ञात्वा कार्यार्थी कार्य साधयेत्।

Those working under a master must know the nature of the master before devoting themselves to work. [The intelligent workers first assess the nature of their master – what kind of man is he; what he wants etc., and then decide how they should work.]

139. धेनो: शीलज्ञ क्षीरं भुङ्क्ते।

Similarly, he who knows the nature of cow enjoys her milk the best way.

140. क्षुद्रे गुह्यप्रकाशन मात्मवान् न कुर्यात्।

Never share your secrets with some one lacking depth of character.

141. आश्रितैरप्यवमनसते मृदुस्वभाव:।

A soft-natured person gets insulted even by his dependents! [A soft-natured person is no asset in the state administration as his/her soft nature would tempt even his/her dependents/ subordinates to defy or insult him or her.]

142. तीक्ष्णदण्ड: सर्वरुद्वेनीयो भवति।

A king who punishes his culprits ruthlessly is hated by all his subjects. [In the stateadministration if a ruler is cruel or sadist, he is unlikely to get any favour from his subjects. On the contrary he will be the target of their hatred.]

143. यथार्ह दण्डकारी स्यात्।

(In continuation of the previous Sutra). Hence the king must punish the culprit judiciously. [Extra hard punishment may make the ruler the butt of his subjects' hatred and extra leniency may make the culprit rather over audacious. Hence the punishment must be just and appropriate.]

144. अल्पसारं श्रुतवन्तपि न बहुमन्यते लोकः।

A frivolous scholar doesn't command respect of the people. [A scholar is expected to be serious and solemn and not frivolous particularly before the people.]

145. अतिभारः पुरुषमवसादयति।

Extra burden of work make the man unhappy and worried. [The king should assign as much work to his assistants as the later is competent enough to finish his normal capacity.]

146. यः संसदि परदोषं शंसति स स्वदोषं प्रख्यापयति।

He who points out other's flaw in the people's court or parliament, draws people's attention to his own inefficiency. [In the people's court the topic of discussion should be confined to the flaws in the system of governance rather than on the individual's inefficiency. He who does so, in fact lowers the stature of that august court.]

147. आत्मनमेव नाशयत्यनात्मवातां कोप:।

The anger of those who are not aware of their own capabilities eventually goes to destroy themselves. [The anger of fools eventually damages their own interest].

148. नास्त्यप्राप्यं सत्यवताम्।

Nothing is inaccessible or unachieveable for those who are endowed with the wealth of truth. [It is an indirect way of asserting that truth makes you achieve all that you want to; for sticking to truth is the greatest wealth in this fey world.]

149. साहसेन न कार्यसिद्धिर्भवति।

Alone courage is not enough to achieve success in one's mission. [Courage is necessary but unless one has knowledge and resources, one is not likely to achieve one's objective.]

150. व्यसानार्तो विरमत्यप्रवेशन।

He who is addicted to vices fails to achieve his objective. [An addicted fellow has his vision clouded by the need of his pet drug which gains the prime importance and not the achievement of the objective. Indirectly it is asserted that the addicted person shouldn't be entrusted with any important responsibility.]

151. नास्त्यनन्तराय: कालविक्षेपे।

One must finish one's job at due time because any delay may not let one complete it at all!

152. असंशयविनाशात् संशयविनाश: श्रेयान्।

The destruction in present is better than destruction in future. [Perish in what you know to be certain destruction than perish in a prolonged confusion. In other words, dying fighting in a battle field is better than accepting defeat and later dying at the scaffold!]

153. अपरधनानि निक्षेप्तु: केवलम् स्वार्थम्।

Discrimination towards other's wealth (or property) is selfishness. [If you have other's wealth in your possession, guard it as if it is your own. Don't discriminate between yours and other's wealth. For that discrimination gives rise to selfishness.]

154. दानं धर्म:।

Charity is religion. [Charity is the essence of the religious faith by the Hindu scriptures. But this charity ought to be shown to the deserving person without any arrogance on the donor's part.]

155. नार्यागतोऽर्थ वद्विपरौतोऽनर्थभाव:।

The uncivllized persons longing for wealth spells doom for human life. [The love for money among the ignorant may set a wrong trend, which many influence even the knowledgeableperson. And this blind love for wealth may lead to destruction for the human life as this is quite infectious.]

156. यो धर्मार्थो न विवर्धयति स कामः।

That resource which doesn't add to one's religious faith, is purely an endeavour to satiate one's carnal desires.

157. तद्विपरीतोऽर्थाभासः।

(In continuation of the previous Sutra) The money that one may get through wrong means is actually no money in reality. [The money earned through illegal means gives one no financial strength as the ill earned money gets spent in the wrong ways only. For example, money earned through gamble may be spent in drinking liquor or in womanizing etc.]

158. ऋजुस्वभावपरो जनेषु दुर्लभः।

A man of simple nature is a rare commodity among men. [Since the people are generally of vile nature, they don't let a simple hearted man survive in society. But if such a man manages tosurvive, obviously such a man will be very rare.]

159. अवमानेनागतमैश्वर्यमवमन्यते साधुः।

He who does not accept the wealth given by an insulting

manner is a real saint. [The real good man or saintly person is he who never cares for wealth and riches even if it is thurst upon him. Any opulence offered to him through an insulting manner is totally unacceptable to him.]

160. बहूनपि गुणानेक दोषो ग्रसति।

Even if one has a single bad quality, it shall nullify all his other good qualities. [A rotten apple injures all its companions.]

161. महात्मना परेण साहसं न कर्तव्यम्।

A great man never relies on other's help while doing a courageous act.

162. कदाचिदपि चरित्रं न लंघेत्।

One must not violate one's basic characteristics.

163. क्षुधर्तो न तृणं चरति सहः।

A hungry lion would never eat grass. [Both the Sutras : the previous one and this one are inter related. Previous Sutra is explained by a glaring example in this Sutra.]

164. प्राणदपि प्रत्ययो रक्षितव्यः।

One must protect one's faith even at the cost of one's life.

165. पिशुन: श्रोता पुत्रदारैरपि त्यज्यते।

He who is given to back-biting is eventually forsaken by one's own wife and son. [Back-biting or criticizing someone at one's back is a vile habit. Even one's close ones can't tolerate it for long.]

166. बालादप्यर्थजातं श्रृणुयात्।

Even children should be fed on meaningful information. [Chanakya says that even the children should be reared on meaningful talks and not on flimsy or fantastical stories. Tell them only such stories as have some useful information.]

167. सत्यमप्यश्रद्धेयं न वदेत्।

If truth be unpalatable or disturbing one's faith, it should not be said. [If any revelation of truth may create disturbance in the listener's faith, it shouldn't be told before that person.]

168. नाल्पदोषाद्‌ बहुगुणस्त्यज्यन्ते।

If a virtuous person has a few bad qualities, discard him owing to those flaws. [Existence of the minor flaws do not make a virtuous person discardable. Neglect his flaws but embrace his virtues.]

169. विपश्चित्स्वपि सुलभा दोष:।

Even the learned persons can make mistakes.

170. नास्ति रत्नमखण्डितम्।

(In continuation of the previous Sutra) Even the most precious gem can have some flaws. [Like the wise may have some weaknesses, the same way the most precious gem may have some flaws.]

171. मर्यादातीतं न कदाचिदपि विश्वसेत्।

Never rely on a person known to transgress the limit of virtues. [Never rely on a person who violates the rules of law or social norms.]

172. अप्रियेण कृतं प्रियमपि द्वेष्यं भवति।

Even a favour done by an enemy can be harmful! [For that favour can prove to be your undoing later on.]

173. नमन्त्यपि तुलाकोटि: कूपोदकक्षयं करोति।

An appliance for drawing water from a well ruins the water by repeatedly bowing down. [Even the bowing of the mean is a forerunner to their intention of looting or deceiving you. So be wary of their showing any respect to you.]

174. सतां मतं नातिक्रमेत्।

Never violate the opinion of the gentlemen. [Gentlemen's opinion conveys their life-long experience truthfully. Hence it should never to violated.]

175. गुणवदाश्रयन्निर्गुणोऽपि गुणी भवति।

Staying with the virtuous makes even the virtue-less person virtuous. [A good company has its indelible impact.]

176. क्षीराश्रितं जलं क्षीरमेव भवति।

The company of milk makes even water as good as milk. [The thought of the previous Sutra is exemplified here through the mixture of water with milk.]

177. मृत्पिण्डोऽपि पाटिलगन्धमुत्पादयति।

Even raw earth (or soil) if it remains in touch with flowers produces fragrance.

178. रजतं कनकसंगात् कनकं भवति।

Silver becomes gold when mixed with gold.

179. उपकर्तर्यपकर्तुमिछत्यबुधः।

A fool acts foul with even those who do him/her good.

180. न पापकर्मणामाक्रोशभयम्।

A sinful person is not afraid of ill-fame.

181. उत्साहवतां शत्रवोऽपि वशीभवन्ति।

Courageous persons overpower even their enemies. [Even if the courageous persons face powerful enemies, they overpower them merely by their dominant courage.]

182. विक्रमधना राजानः।

A king becomes rich with his valourous attitude.

183. नास्त्यलसस्यैहकायुष्यिकम्।

There is no present or future for a lazy person.

184. निरुत्साहाद् दैवं पतति।

Absence of enthusiasm ruins even his own fortune (bestowed by God).

185. मत्स्यार्थीव जलमुपयुज्यार्थं गृह्णीयात्।

Dire into water and draw out benefits like a fisher. [Enter unto troubles fearlessly if one wants to convert a problem into an opportunity.]

186. अविश्वस्तेषु विश्वासो न कर्तव्यः।

Never rely on someone who is a known betrayer.

187. विषं विषमेव सर्वकालम्।

Poison is poison in all circumstances.

188. अर्थ समादाने वैरिणां संग एव न कर्तव्यः।

While collecting money leave the enemies out.

189. अर्थसिद्धौ वैरिणं न विश्वसेत्।

Never trust your adversaries while endeavouring to achieve your target.

190. अर्थाधीन एव नियतसम्बन्धः।

Every relationship is linked with some common advantage (to be achieved).

191. शत्रुरिप सुतः सखा रक्षितव्यः।

Protect the son of even enemy if he becomes your friend. [Since you and your enemy-king's son's objective is common

– removing that king from the throne – treat his son as your friend.]

192. यावच्छत्रोश्छिद्रं तावद् बद्धहस्तेन वा स्कन्धेन वा बाह्य:।

Keep your enemy deceived by your artificial behaviour till you find his weaknesses.

193. शत्रुछिद्रे प्रहरेत्।

Attack on the weakness of your enemy. [That is, your strategy should be to first find your enemy's weaknesses and attack on them.]

194. आत्मछिद्रं न प्रकाशयेत।

Never disclose your weakness to anyone.

195. छिद्रप्रहारिण: शत्रव:।

Enemies always targets your weaknesses. [Hence don't get them revealed at all.]

196. हस्तगतमपि शत्रुं न विश्वसेद्।

Never rely on enemy even when you have captured him/her.

197. स्वजनस्य दुर्वृत्तं निवारयेत्।

Try to remove the flaws in your close one's character. [Because these flaws make your defence penetrable.]

198. स्वजनावमोनोऽपि मनस्विनां दु:खमावहति:।

Strong-willed (or character) persons get saddened when their close ones are insulted. [Insult to the close ones creates wound in the heart of the strong-willed persons because that belittles their reputation.]

199. एकांगदोष: पुरुषमवसादयति।

One feels agony even if one part of one's body has some defect.

200. शत्रुंजयति सुवृत्तता।

Only good or noble habits win the enemies.

201. मिकृतिप्रिया नीचा:।

A mean fellow is ever troublesome for a noble man.

202. नीचस्य मतिर्न दातव्या।

No advice should be given to the vile persons. [For they'll never heed to it.]

203. तेषुविश्वासो न कर्त्तव्य: ।

Therefore, such persons (mischief mongers) should never be relied upon.

204. सुपूजितोऽपि दुर्जन: पीडयत्येव।

Even if honoured, a mischief-monger will only give trouble. [Hence such person should never be honoured, no matter whatever be their value!]

205. चन्दनानपि दावोऽग्निर्दहत्येव।

The forest five burns even the priced wood like sandalwood etc.

206. कदाऽपि पुरुषं नावमन्येत्।

Never insult a noble man.

207. क्षन्तव्यमिति पुरुषं न बाधेत्।

Never make a pardonable person [i.e. he whose folly is pardonable] sad.

208. भर्त्राधिकं रहस्ययुक्तं वक्तुमिच्छन्त्यबुद्धय:।

Only fools reveal the secrets told to them by their masters in privacy.

209. अनुरागस्तु फलेन सूच्यते।

Affection is revealed not by words but by action. [Love doesn't need words to reveal itself since lover's gestures and actions reveal it automatically.]

210. आज्ञाफलमैश्वर्यम्।

Opulence's effect is revealed by [the compliance of] its order.

211. दातव्यमपि बलिश: क्लेशेन दास्यति।

Fools give trouble to even their benefactors.

212. महदैश्वर्यं प्राप्याप्यधृतिमान् विनश्यति:।

The impatient persons perish even when coming in great wealth and opulence. [Since their impatience would make them indulge so recklessly in pleasure that their health would be severely damaged and in consequence they shall die.]

213. नास्त्यधृतैरैहिकामामुष्मिकम्।

The impatient persons have no present or future. [No present because he would be too reckless in ruining his health and no future for he may not survive for long.]

214. न दुर्जनैः सह संसर्गः कर्तव्यः।

Always avoid company of the rogues.

215. शौण्डहस्तगतं पयोऽप्यवमन्यते।

Even milk is unacceptable if given by a drunkard. [Be wary of the apparently noble gesture of a bad person.]

216. कार्यसंकटेष्वर्थव्यवसायिनी बुद्धिः।

Intelligent persons detect their benefit even amdist crisis. [If you have intelligence, you'll convert a crisis also into an opportunity and derive some benefit for yourself.]

217. मितभोजनं स्वास्थ्यम्।

Frugal diet is the key to good health.

218. पथ्यमपथ्यम् वाऽजीर्णे नाश्नीयत्।

If heavy food causes dyspepsia avoid taking even easily digestible food.

219. जीर्णभोजिनं व्याधिर्नोपि सर्पितः।

Properly disgested food causes no illness.

220. जीर्णशरीरे वर्धमानं व्याधिं नोपेक्ष्येत्।

Never neglect even a minor ailment in the weak or emaciated body.

221. अजीर्णे भोजनं दुःखम्।

Eating any food in dyspepsia cause trouble.

222. शत्रोरपि विशिष्यते व्याधिः।

Disease is more dangerous than enemy.

223. दानं निधनमनुगामि।

Donation should be made according to once's capacity.

224. पदुतरे तृष्णापरे सुलभमतिसन्धानम्।

It is only the cunning and greedy persons who try to be extra intimate for no apparent reason.

225. तृष्णया मतिश्छाद्यते।

Greed clouds one's intelligence.

226. कार्यबहुत्वे बहफलमायतिकं कुर्यात्।

If one has many jobs in hand, do that first which fetches maximum benefit.

227. स्वयमेवावस्कन्नं कार्यं निरीक्षेत्।

Revise the wrongly done job by you or others personally. [Never trust a wrongly done job to any one else but check yourself.]

228. मूर्खेषु साहसं नियतम्।

Fools are by nature foolhardy.

229. मूर्खेषु विवादो न कर्त्तव्यः।

Never bandy words with fools.

230. मूर्खेषु मूर्खवत् कथ्येत्।

Converse with fools in their own language.

231. आयसैरावसं छेद्यम्।

Iron gets cut by iron only. [Behave with fools the way they behave.]

232. नास्त्यधीमतः सखा।

Fools have no friend.

233. धर्मेणः धार्यते लोकः।

One must follow one's Dharma in this world. [When all follow their Dharma the human society rests in peace.]

234. प्रेतमपि धर्माधर्मावनुगच्छतः।

Even the ghosts and spirits follow their Dharma. [Not only in this world, even after death one must stick to one's Dharma in observing obsequies, last rites etc.]

235. दया धर्मस्य जन्मभूमिः।

The birth place (root) of Dharma is compassion (for others).

236. धर्ममूले सत्यदाने।

An honest donation is the root of Dharma.

237. धर्मेण जयति लोकान्।

He who follows his Dharma truthfully scores victory in all his worldly endeavours. [Since he remains firm on his faith, he gets honour from everybody and faces no trouble in discharging his worldly duties as well.]

238. मृत्युरपि धर्मिष्ठं रक्षति।

Even death protects such a person sticking to his faith firmly. [As he gets renown even after his death.]

239. तद्विपरीतं पापं यत्र प्रसज्यते तत्र।

However those who act contrary to this dictate [that is, who don't stick to their faith] spread sin and cause great dishonour to Dharma.

240. उपस्थितविनाशानां प्रकृत्याकारेण लक्ष्यते।

Impending doom is conveyed by Nature's indications.

241. आत्मविनाशं सूचचत्यधर्मबुद्धिः।

When one acts contrary to one's religious tenets, it indicates impending self-destruction.

242. पिशुनवादिनो न रहस्यम्।

Never disclose your secrets to a back-biter.

243. पर रहस्यं नैव श्रोतव्यं।

Never try to know other's secret. [The previous Sutra and this Sutra are both in fact complementary to each other.]

244. वल्लभस्य कारकत्वमधर्म युक्तम्।

The master must not be over-friendly with his or her subordinates, as the later, then, would behave quite contemptuously, crossing the limits of propriety.

245. स्वजने स्वतिक्रमो न कर्त्तव्यः।

One should not insult or show contempt to one's closeness.

246. माताऽपि दुष्टा त्याज्या।

Desert your mother even, if she is wicked or rogue.

247. स्वहस्तोऽपि विषदिग्धश्छेद्यः।

Cut off even your hand if it is inflicted with poison. [Like the important part of your body should be cut off if afflicted, the same way get rid of the rogues from society, no matter how close or dear they may be to you.]

248. परोऽपि च हितो बन्धुः।

If a stranger is your well-wisher, treat him or her like your sibling.

249. कक्षादत्यौषधं गृह्यते।

Even the dried jungle can give you a herbal medicine. [If you can get something that heals you from even the most unexpected or wretched source, get it without any hesitation.]

250. नास्ते चौरेषु विश्वासः।

Never rely on the thieves.

251. अप्रतीकारेष्वनादरो न कर्तव्यः।

Never ignore your enemy even if he appears indifferent. [One should never ignore one's enemy no matter how indifferent he (or she) may pretend to be; for cloaking under the indifference he may be lurking his sinister designs.]

252. व्यसनं मनागपि बधते।

Even a minor addiction can give you trouble (some time).

Amass wealth deeming oneself to be immortal. [Chanakya says that one must amass wealth sparing no efforts. Don't slacken your efforts thinking that you may not survive long to enjoy it.]

254. अर्थवानम् सर्वलोकस्य बहुमतः।

The whole world respects the wealthy (or resourceful person).

255. महेन्दयष्यर्थहीनं न बहु मन्यते लोकः।

The world doesn't respect even a king if he has no wealth (or resources).

256. दारिद्रयं खलु पुरुषस्य जीवितं मरणम्।

Suffering poverty is like dying even though you are alive.

257. विरूपोऽर्थवान सुरूपः।

Money can make even an ugly person good looking.

258. अदातारमप्यर्थवन्तर्थिनो न त्यजन्ति।

The beggars won't spare even a miserly or stingy moneyed man.

259. अकुलीनोऽपि धनी कुली कुलीनाद्विशिष्ट:।

A scion from an aristocratic family with no money is better than a moneyed man from a lowly family.

260. नास्त्यवमानभयमनार्यस्य।

A mean person is not scared of his insult.

261. न चेतनवतां वृत्तिभयम्।

Skilled persons are not afraid of losing their livelihood.

262. न जितेन्द्रियाणां विषयभयम्।

Those who have control over their senses are not afraid of their indulgence in sensual delights.

263. न कृतार्थानां मरणभयम्।

The righteous have no fear of death.

264. कस्यचिदर्थं स्वमिव मन्यते साधु:।

A gentleman deems everyone's wealth as his very own. [That is, a gentleman never allows any wealth to be wasted and preserves it as if it belongs to him only. The idea is that he who has anyone else's wealth in one's possession must guard it as if it is his own.]

265. परविभवेष्वादरो न कर्तव्यः।

One should never covet other's wealth or opulence.

266. परविभेष्वादऽरोपि नाशमूलम्।

Greed for other's wealth is the root of one's doom. [He who covets other's wealth eventually causes his doom because in that lust his all activities will be centred on other's wealth. He may not do something by his own effort. And such a man has no holds barred for stooping low. Thus he creates his passage on his own fall.]

267. अल्पमपि पर द्रव्यं न हर्तव्यम्।

One shouldn't steal even the smallest amount belonging to others.

268. परद्रव्यापहरणमात्मद्रव्यनाशहेतुः।

Usurping other's wealth or property (or money) is a sure way of destroying one's own money. [For a thief can't remain free forever. And when he is caught he would not only be forced to surrender the stolen wealth but shall be compelled to pay punishment etc., which may finish all the money he has, eventually.]

269. न चौर्यात्परं मृत्युपाश:।

It is better to die than indulge in stealing.

270. यवागूरपि प्राणधारिणं करोति लोके।

One can survive by eating only a meal of parched grain power (Sattoo). [Hence one shouldn't covet for other's money.]

271. न मृतस्यौषधं प्रयोजनम्।

A dead man needs no medicine.

272. समकाले स्वयमपि प्रभुत्वस्य प्रयोजनं भवित।

Ensuring one's supremacy in a peace-time itself becomes the ever-lasting objective.

273. नीचस्य विद्या: पापकर्मणि योजयन्ति।

The mean-minded ever use their education in the sinful activities.

274. पय:पानमपि विषवर्धन भुजंगस्य नामृतं स्यात्।

Feeding a snake on milk will only enhance the poison in it and shall not create any nectar. [Making the mean strong will not purify their character. Only their meanness will be further augmented.]

275. न हि धन्यसमो ह्यर्थः।

There is no wealth like having food-grains. [Since eating food is the ultimate necessity for survival, having food-grain is the ultimate wealth.]

276. न क्षुधसमः शत्रुः।

There is no deadlier enemy than facing hunger.

277. अकृतेर्नियताक्षुत्।

To die of hunger is writ large in the destiny of the work-shirker, lazy persons.

278. नास्त्यभक्ष्यं क्षुधितस्य।

Nothing is uneatable for a hungry man.

279. इन्द्रियाणि जरावशं कुर्वन्ति।

(Over) Indulgence in sensory pleasures expedites the onset of the old age.

280. सानुक्रोशं भर्तारमाजीवेत्।

He who is considerate to his servants weal and woe really deserves their services.

281. लुब्धसेवी पावकेच्छया खद्योतं धमति।

The servant of a tough (inconsiderate) master serves his master as though someone is trying to set fire in the wood by throwing on them the tuff glow-worms (instead of the fire-lings). [That is, serving a heartless master is akin to trying to set fire by using glow-worm on the wood. Like this is a futile attempt, so is servant's service to a heartless master.]

282. विशेषज्ञ स्वामिनमाश्रयेत्।

One must always seek shelter of a considerate and sensitive master.

283. पुरुषस्य मैथुनं जारा।

A man ages fast if he copulates more.

284. स्त्रीणां अमैथुनं जारा।

A woman ages fast if she doesn't indulge in copulation.

285. न नीचोत्तमयोर्विवाहः।

A matrimonial alliance must be between the persons of matching status and nature. A man with lofty ideals must not marry a mean-minded girl.

286. अगम्भयागमनादायुर्यवा: पुण्यानि क्षीयन्ते।

Copulation with a woman of prohibitive category makes a man lose fast his age, glory and the merits of youth.

287. नास्त्यहंकर समः शत्रुः।

Arrogance is one's greatest enemy.

288. संसदि शत्रु न परिक्रोशेत्।

Never show your anger on your enemy at a public conference. [Public display of one's emotion on any individual is not correct as it shifts the focus of the conference to personal issue from an issue of public interest.]

289. शत्रुव्यसनं श्रवणसुखम्।

Hearing derogatory things about one's enemy gives much pleasure.

290. अधनस्य बुद्धिर्न विद्यते।

A pauper lacks wisdom.

291. हितमप्यधनस्य वाक्य न श्रृणोति।

No body listens to a wise advice given by a pauper. [A pauper commands no respect even though he (or she) be very intelligent or wise. Hence no one cares for his advice, no matter how sane he is.]

292. अधन: स्वभार्ययाब्ययमन्यते।

A money-less person gets insulted by his own wife. [Since such a person is unlikely to provide funds for running the house, he will have to face frequent insult from his wife.]

293. पुष्पहीनं सहकारमपि नोपासते भ्रमरा:।

Bees desert even a flowerless mango tree. [Here flowerless means it has no hope of getting any fruit.]

294. विद्या धनमधनानाम्।

The wealth of the paupers is their education (or knowledge).

295. विद्या चौरैरपि न ग्राह्या।

Thieves can't steal one's education (or knowledge).

296. विद्या ख्यापिता ख्याति:।

Education (knowledge) spreads one's fame.

297. यश: शरीरं न विनश्यति।

One's fame never gets destroyed.

298. य: परार्थमुपसर्पति स सत्पुरुष:।

He who comes ahead for other's benefit is the real man.

299. इन्द्रियाणां प्रशम शास्त्रम्।

That knowledge which teaches one to keep one's senses under control is the real knowledge.

300. अशास्त्राकार्यवृत्तौ शास्त्राकुशं निवारयति।

When evil spreads, that knowledge which teaches to control one's senses, shows its dominance.

301. नीचस्य विद्या नोपेतव्या।

The knowledge of the mean should never be accepted.

302. म्लेच्छभाषण न शिक्षेत्।

The language of the Mlechchha (barbarians) should never be learnt. [Because it is a language full of vile vocabulary.]

303. म्लेच्छानामपि सुवृत्तं ग्राह्यम्।

The good qualities of the barbarians can be adopted (in one's life-style).

304. गुणे न मत्सर: कार्य:।

Never be lazy in learning (or adopting) good qualities.

305. शत्रोरपि सुगुणो ग्राह्य:।

The good qualities of an enemy should be taken (or adopted).

306. विषादप्यमृतं ग्राह्यम्।

If even poison has traces of nectar, it should be taken from it.

307. अवस्थया पुरुष: सम्मान्यते।

One gets respect due to one's position. [One gets position in society due to doing one's duties well which in turn gives one respect.]

308. स्थान एव नरा पूज्यन्ते।

A man is adored by the qualities he possesses.

309. आर्यवृत्तमनुतिष्ठेत्।

Always try to maintain your best behaviour.

310. कदापि मर्यादां नातिमेत्।

Never transgress your limits.

311. नास्त्यर्ध पुरुष रत्नस्य।

Man is such a gem which can not be evaluated. [Man is a bundle of infinite qualities. No one knows when they would glow. Hence his real worth cannot be evaluated in worldly terms.]

312. न स्त्रीरत्नसमं रत्नम्।

Nor there is anything as precious as a woman is. [She is also an incomparable gem.]

313. सुदुर्लभं रत्नम्।

It is indeed rare to get a precious gem. [Impliedly a real man and woman are rare gems.]

314. अयशो भयं भयेषु।

Ill-fame is the deadliest fear (for a man). [What hurts most a genuine man is infamy. This is the dealiest fear for such persons.]

315. नास्त्यलसस्य शास्त्रागमः।

A lazy or callous man can never learn scriptures.

316. न स्त्रैण स्वर्गाप्तिर्धर्मकृत्यं च।

An effeminate man (or a man ever hankering after women in his lust) can never hope to complete any religious duty or go to heaven.

317. स्त्रियोऽपि स्त्रैणमवमन्यते।

Even a woman abhors an effeminate man.

318. न पुष्पार्थी सिञ्चति शुष्कतरुम्।

A man desiring to get flowers never irrigates a dry plant.

319. अद्रव्यप्रयत्नो बालुकाक्वथानादनन्यः।

Doing a job without any investment of money is tantamount to trying to squeeze out oil from sand. [That is futile.]

320. न महाजनहासः कर्त्तव्यः।

Never make great persons the butt of ridicule. [That is, always treat them with honour.]

321. कार्यसम्पदं निमित्तानि सूचयन्ति।

The indications of doing a job give the advance information about its eventual success or failure.

322. नक्षत्रादि निमित्तानि विशेषयन्ति।

The asterisms or planets can also predict about failure or success in the contemplated job.

323. न त्वरितस्य नक्षत्रपरीक्षा।

But the one desirous of getting success in one's effort quickly doesn't wait for examining the position of asterisms or planets.

324. परिचये दोषा न छाद्यन्ते।

Mere introduction doesn't reveal one's flaws or deficiencies.

325. स्वयमशुद्धः परानाशंकते।

He who is himself impure, worries most about others impurity.

326. स्वभावो दुरतिक्रमः।

One's basic nature cannot be altered.

327. अपराधनुरूपो दण्ड:।

The awarded punishment must commensurate with the committed crime.

328. कथानुरूपं प्रतिवचनम्।

The counter-comment must conform to the basic remark.

329. विभवानुरूपमाभरणम्।

One must wear dress or ornaments according to his opulence level.

330. कुलानुरूपं वृत्तम्।

One's character must conform to the level of reputation of his clan.

331. कार्यानुरूप: प्रयत्न:।

Efforts must measure according to the need of the job undertaken.

232. नास्त्यधीमत: सखा।

Donation must be made according to the need of the receiver.

333- वयोऽनुरूप: वेष: ।

One's dress must befit his age.

334- स्वाम्यनुकूलो भृत्य: ।

The servant must always follow the order of his master.

335- गुरुवशानुवर्ती शिष्य: ।

The disciple must always follow his (or her) mentor's commands.

336. भर्तृशानुवर्तिनी भार्या।

A wife must behave according to her husband's desires.

337- पितृवशानुवर्ती पुत्र: ।

A son must always be obedient to his father.

338. अत्युपचार: शंकितव्य: ।

Observance of excessive formality engenders suspicion (about the observer's true intentions).

339. स्वामिनमेवानुवर्तेत्।

An employee must follow the employer's demands.

340. मातृताडितो वत्सो मातरमेवानुरोदिति।

A child punished by his mother weeps only before her. [A child never complains his mother's behaviour before anyone because he never doubts the sincerity of his mother about his wellbeing.]

341. स्नेहवत् स्वल्पो हि रोष:।

Even the wrath of the well-wishers (like parents or the Guru) is always laced with affection. [Because they act hard to have the weakness in their ward or child's behaviours duly rectified.]

342. आत्मछिद्रं न पश्यति परिछिद्रमेव पश्यति बालिश:।

Only a fool concentrates on finding faults in others and not in his own self.

343. सोपचार: कैतव:।

The scoundrels serve others with dishonest intentions.

344. काम्यैर्विशेषैरूपचरणमुपचार:।

[In continuation to the previous Sutra] The scoundrels show their services through offering gifts the master specially likes.

345. चिरपरिचितानामत्युपचार: शंकितव्य:।

The display of extra formality by the well-known person evokes a (genuine) suspicious. [Why must a well-known person show such excessive formality?]

346. गौर्दुष्करा श्वसहस्त्रादेकाकिनी श्रेयसी।

An irritable or foul-tempered cow is better than having a thousand dogs (at one's gate).

347. श्वो मयूरादद्य कपोतो वर:।

Today's pigeon is better than having a peacock of tomorrow. [This is akin to the English proverb: one in hand is better than two in the luck.]

348. अतिसंगो दोषामुत्पादयति।

Extra affection breads weaknesses. [It is akin to the English proverb: familiarity breads contempt.]

349. सर्व जयत्यक्रोध:।

He who controls his anger totally wins over everyone.

350. यद्यपकारिणि कोपः कोपे कोप एवं कर्तव्यः।

Express your anger only after the wrong doer expresses his anger at being exposed. [Let the wrong-doer first come up with resentment (or anger) at being exposed, then you must show your anger. This way you'd not let him find any excuse to escape.]

351. मतिमत्सु मूर्खमित्रगुरुवल्लभेषु विवादो न कर्तव्यः।

Never bandy words with the wise, fools, friends, mentor and master.

352. नस्त्यपिशाचमैश्वर्यम्।

Opulence is not devoid of evils. [With extra opulence or money, some evils do creep in. Hence, one must be cautious about them.]

353. नास्ति धनवतां शुभकर्मसुश्रमः।

The rich never (selflessly) contribute in noble work. [For they always seek their financial gain in whatever they do.]

354. नास्ति गतिश्रमो यानवताम्।

Those who depend upon vehicles (for their movement) never exert to walk on foot. [And this way, they never get the benefit of walking on foot.]

355- अलौहमयं निगडं कलत्रम्।

A wife is an iron-less chain (round the husband's feet). [Getting a wife entails many duties and hence a man doesn't remain totally free anymore.]

356. यो चरित्रकुशल: सतस्मिन योत्तकव्य:।

He who excels in a particular field must be given a job of that field only.

357- दुष्टकलत्रंयनास्विनाँ शरीरकर्शनम्।

Scholars deem a rogue wife to be a constant cause of sorrow.

358. अप्रमत्तो दारान्निरीक्षेत्।

(Hence) Examine the potential wife with utmost care.

359- स्त्रीषु किञ्चिदपि न विश्वसेत्।

Never trust a woman (even in the least). [The implied meaning is directed towards bad or characterless women.]

360. न समाधि स्त्रीषु लोकज्ञता च।

Women in general lack in being versed in social etiquette

and discretionary wisdom.

361. गुरुणां माता गरीयसी।

One's mother is one's best teacher.

362. सर्ववस्थासु माता भर्तव्या।

Take care of your mother in all conditions devotedly.

363. वैदुष्यमलंकारेणाच्छाद्यते।

Outward decoration hides one's erudite knowledge. [Outwardly well decorated scholar doesn't seem what he is owing to the distracting ornamentation of the person. Chanakya says that a scholar shouldn't be so decoratively dressed.]

364. स्त्रीणां भूषणं लज्जा।

Shyness or modesty is the jewel of women.

365. विप्राणां भूषणं वेदः।

(Knowledge of the) Vedas represent intelligent brahman's jewel.

366. सर्वेषां भूषणं धर्मः।

Dharma is the real jewel of everyone. [He who knows his duties and responsibilities well is like a real gem in the society.]

367. अनुपद्रवं देशभावसेत।

Always stay in a country (or place) free of riots and anarchy.

368. साधु जन बहुलो देशः।

The really dwellable country is that which has majority of noble men.

369. राज्ञो भेतव्यं सार्वकालं।

One should always be afraid of one's king.

370. न राज्ञः परं देवतम्।

For no deities is more adorable than the king. [As the king is the top deity.]

371. सुदूरमपि दहति राजवन्हिः।

The royal wrath is a strong fire that burns the evils of even a far-off region.

372. रिक्तहस्तो न राजानमभिगच्छेत्।

Never go to your king with empty hands. [That is one must always carry gift for one's king.]

373- गुरुं च दैवं च।

Never also go to your Guru or temple of the deity with empty hands.

374- कुटुम्बिनो भेतव्यम्।

Never bear a grudge for the royal family.

375- गन्तव्यं च सदा राजकुलम्।

Visit the royal family regularly. [Maintaining the contact with the royal family has a lot of hidden advantages.]

376. राजपुरुषैः सम्बन्धं कुर्यात्।

Maintain cordial relations with the royal personages.

377- राजदासी न सेवितव्या।

Never increase intimacy with the royal maid servant.

378. न चक्षुषाऽपि राजातं निरीक्षेत्।

Never look in the eyes of the king while standing before

him.

379. पुत्रे गुणवति कुटुम्बिन: स्वर्ग:।

A virtuous scion of a family makes all his family members happy. [An able son of the family makes its all members live happily due to his achievements. (However, this is true with only joint family system).]

380. पुत्रा: विद्यानां पार गमयितव्या।

(Hence) One must make his son well-versed in a variety of fields and subjects.

381. जनपदार्थ ग्रामं त्यजेत्।

Sacrifice a village for ensuring a region's or country's welfare.

382. ग्रामार्थ कुटुम्बं त्यजेत्।

Sacrifice a family for ensuring a village's welfare.

383. अतिलाभ: पुत्रलाभ:।

Begetting a son brings the best blessings.

384. दुर्गति: पितरौ रक्षित स पुत्र:।

He is the real son who protects his parents from all troubles.

385. कुलं प्रख्यापयति पुत्रः।

An able son brings glory to the entire family.

386. नानपत्यस्य स्वर्गः।

A son-less person is denied the entry into heaven. [This is an old Indian belief.]

387. या प्रसूते सा भार्या।

She who gives a son is the real wife.

388. तीर्थसमवाये पुत्रवतीमनुगच्छेत्।

The king must go to that queen (following her productive period) who has given him a son.

389. सतीर्थगमनाद् ब्रह्मचर्य नश्यति।

One loses one's potency if one copulates with a woman under menstruation.

390. न परक्षेत्रे बीज विनिक्षिपेत्।

Never throw your seed into a field which is not yours.

391. पुत्रर्था हि स्त्रियः।

The women are meant to produce son.

392. स्वदासी परिग्रहो हि दासभावः।

Having sex with your maid servant is tantamount to becoming their servant.

393. उपस्थितविनाशः पथ्यवाक्यं न श्रृणोति।

The onset of doom doesn't let the potential victim heed to any advice.

394. नास्ति देहिनां सुखदुःखभावः।

Pain and pleasure (or woe and weal) go hand in hand in the life of the mortal beings.

395. मातरमिव वत्साः सुखदुःखानि कर्तारमेवानुगच्छन्ति।

Like children follow their mother, so do pain and pleasure follow the mortal beings.

396. तिलमात्रप्युपकारं शैलषमन्यते साधुः।

A gentleman deems a mole-like obligation as big as a

mountain. [A gentleman always recognizes an act of gratitude and also tries to repay it ten times more than its real wroth.]

397. उपकारोऽनार्येष्वकर्तव्यः।

Never oblige a mean person. [For he or she will never even deem it to be an obligation.]

398. प्रत्युपकारभयादनार्यः शत्रुर्भवति।

A mean person never deems an obligation to be a favour. On the contrary, such act makes him or her your enemy. [Because it hurts his or her ego.]

399. स्वल्पमप्युपकारकृते प्रत्युपकार कर्तुमार्यो स्वपिति।

A gentleman doesn't feel satisfied till he has repaid even a smallest obligation.

400. न कदाऽपि देवताऽवमन्तव्या।

Never dishonouor (or insult) the deities.

402. चक्षुर्हि शरीरिणां नेता।

There is no light better than the light which makes eyes see things.

402. चक्षुर्हि शरीरिणां नेता।

Eyes are the leader of the body of the mortal beings. [It is eyes that guide man. Without them nothing can be seen. Hence, they guide the life of mortal beings in this way.]

403. अपचक्षुः क शरीरेण।

A body is useless without the eyes. [Without eyes one can't do his own work.]

404. नाप्सु मूत्रं कुर्यात्।

Never piss while in water. [This way you pollute the water and makes it unusable by others. Hence never piss while in water.]

405. न नग्नो जलं प्रविशेत्।

Never enter water naked.

406. यथा शरीरं तथा ज्ञानम्।

As is one's body, so is one's knowledge. [Deem here the body as the society and you as its member. One gets the knowledge as one's society is constituted. Consequently if you are robust you have a lot of knowledge; if deprived of knowledge you will have an emaciated body.]

407. यथा बुद्धिस्तथा विभवः।

One's opulence or prosperity is directly proportional to one's knowledge. [Here knowledge means the worldliwiseness. The more worldliwise you are, the more riches you will get.]

408. अग्नावाग्निं न निक्षिपेत्।

Never add fire to (the raging) fire. [That is, don't fuel one's anger all the more. Never treat an angry man with more wrath. Treat him calmly. Anger is like fire. Hence don't add fire to the raging fire.]

409. तपस्विनः पूजनीया।

Ascetics are always adorable. [Ascetics are those that renounce the world and do penance which make them very pious and pure. Hence they should be adored.]

410. परदारान् न गच्छेत्।

Never have sex with woman who is not yours.

411. अन्नदानं भ्रणहत्यामपि मार्ष्टि।

Donation of food grain to a hungry person is the greatest donation or act of charity and killing a being in the embryo form is the most heinous crime. The merit of the former form of charity nullify the sin in the later form of crime. [That is, both the acts – charity of food grains and causing foeticide – just balance each other. Impliedly if one has committed foeticide, one can't get over this stigma by donating food grain to a hungry man.]

412. न वेदवाह्यो धर्मः।

Religion or knowledge of Dharma is very much part of the Veda teaching. [The dictates of our Dharma also have their origin in the knowledge of the Vedas. Dharma is not learnt from other sources; it is the Vedas which define Dharma.]

413. कदाचिदपि धर्मं निषेवेत्।

One should act according to one's Dharma [if not always than] at least occasionally. [Although one should always act according to one's Dharma, yet if it is not possible for some reason, at least for some time one should do it, so that one knows what is one's basic duties and responsibilities.]

414. स्वर्गं नयति सुनृतम्।

Honest conduct ensures one's place in heaven. [He who is honest and truthful, not only gets honoured in the world but also get the best dwelling place post-death.]

415. नास्ति सत्यात्परं तपः।

No penance is more merit-bestowing than honestly

416. सत्यं स्वर्गस्य साधनम्।

Sticking to truth is the sure means to gain heaven.

417. सत्येन धार्यते लोकः।

Truthfulness makes the world servive. [The orderliness of the world owes its stability to adherence to truth only. Because truth makes the human society survive and progress.]

418. सत्याद् देवो वर्षति।

Truthfulness makes even the deities happy.

419. नानृतात्पातकं परम्।

No sin is more deadlier than speaking lies.

420. न मीमास्यः गुरवः।

Never criticize your seniors or elders [like your Guru and parents].

421. खलत्वं नोपेयात्।

Never accept any wicked means to achieve your aim. [Follow always the noble path, come what may.]

422. नास्ति खलस्य मित्रम्।

The wicked have no friends. [No one wants to befriend wicked persons because the wicked have no consideration for any one.]

423. लोकयात्रा दरिदं बाधते।

The paupers get no relief in traversing their worldly life. [For them every minute's survival is an ordeal.]

424. अतिशूरो दानशूरः।

A man indulging in charity is really the brave man. [Because in charity you sacrifice some of your necessities to make the needy one happy. This is surely an act of highest bravery.]

425. गुरुदेवब्राह्मणेषु भक्तिर्भूषणम्।

Have devotion to your Guru, Deity and Brahmans. This type of devotion is the crown-jewel of all devotions.

426. सर्वस्य भूषणं विनयः।

Humility is the crowinging virtue of all.

427. अकुलीनोऽपि विनीतः कुलीनाद्विशिष्टः।

A polite but a person of low origin is better than an impolite person of an aristocratic family. [Birth in any family is the act of God. You have no control over your birth in any family – well known or ignoble. But after birth you can and must develop humility in your character so as to get admiration of your society.]

428. आचारादायुर्वर्धते कीर्तिश्च।

Age and fame get enhanced by good conduct. [Your good conduct will no doubt make you famous; you will also enhance your health because good conduct also help you to remain fit and healthy.]

429. प्रियमप्यहितं न वक्तव्यम्।

The idea which is soothing to listen but not good in practice should not be uttered.

430. बहुजनविरुद्धमेकं नानुवर्तेत्।

Don't follow one and desert many. [This is the basic concept of democracy which Chanakya avers. For many can't be wrong while one may be.]

431. न दुर्जनेषु भागधेयः कर्त्तव्यः।

Enter into no partnership with dishonest or crafty person.

432. न कृतार्थेषु नीचेषु सम्बन्धः।

Even if they be lucky, don't maintain relationship with crafty persons. [No matter how they are favoured by their luck, any association with the crafty persons will give you only bad name. So avoid their company even if a possible prosperity in their association may tempt you.]

433. ऋणशत्रु व्याधिर्निविशेषः कर्तव्यः।

Always attempt to root out loan, enemy and diseases. [For even if a trace of those survives, it may develop into a major trouble. So don't let them survive at all.]

434. भूत्यादुर्तनं पुरुषस्य रसायनम्।

The elixir for a man's life is affluence and prosperity. [Physical comforts and financial security make one remain fit and healthy as they act as an elixir.]

435. नार्थिष्वज्ञा कार्या।

A beggar (or some one begging for some favour) should not be insulted (or shown contempt to).

436. दुष्करं कर्म कारयित्वा कर्तारवमवमन्यते नीचः।

A mean-minded person, makes an expert suffer by putting

before him a very difficult job. [The mean always try to trouble the others. They trouble them also who try to work good results for the former. The mean never care to admit anyone's superiority and always try to belittle others achievement.]

437. नाकृतज्ञस्य नरकान्निवर्तनम्।

There is no place except hell (to go) for an ungrateful person. [Ungratefulness is such a sin that an ungrateful has nowhere to go but hell.]

438. जिह्वाऽऽयत्तौ वृद्धिविनाशौ।

One's development or destruction depends very much upon one's tongue (or speech).

439. विषामृतयोराकरो जिह्वा।

One's tongue (or speech) can be the source of poison or nectar. [For if one is guarded in his speech, one will get nectar; if not, then poison.]

440. प्रियवादिनो न शत्रुः।

A man with a sweet tongue has no enemy.

441. स्तुता अपि देवतास्तुस्यन्ति।

Even the gods become happy with a prayer (or their praise).

442. अनृतमपि दुर्वचनं चिरं तिष्ठति।

Even the baseless foul remark remains long in one's memory.

443. राजद्विष्टं न च वक्तव्यम्।

Allegations must not be made against the king.

444. श्रुतिसुखात् कोकिलालापातुष्यन्ति।

Those who love the pleasure of listening sweet notes get satisfied with the cooing of the cuckoo.

445. स्वधर्महेतुः सत्पुरुषः।

Gentlemen's behaviour reveals the purpose of their religious faith. [For example if the purpose of any faith is helping others, the real followers of that faith will reveal it through their behaviour.]

446. नास्त्यर्थिनो गौरवम्।

Excessive love for money gives one no glory. [Like the misers who love their money excessively are generally denounced by their society.]

447. स्त्रीणां भूषणं सौभाग्यम्।

Good-luck (remaining married with husband alive) is the best jewel for women.

448. शत्रेरपि न पातनीया वृत्तिः।

Even the enemy's source of income shouldn't be destroyed.

449. अप्रयत्नोदकं क्षेत्रम्।

That place should be one's home/place of stay where the source of water be available without much effort. [In a tropical country like India water is very essential for survival. If one has to make extreme efforts for getting it, there is no sense in staying at that place.]

450. एरण्डमवलम्ब्य कुञ्जरं न कोपयेत।

Never invite the wrath of an elephant (the powerful) on getting the support of an Eirand (a weaktree). [Inviting the wrath of the powerful on the support of a weak ally is not prudent.]

451. अतिप्रवृद्धा शाल्मली वरणस्तम्भो न भवति।

No matter how old is the 'Saal' tree, it can't be used to tie an elephant to it. [A 'Saal' tree is normally quite sturdy and strong but when withered with age it can no more be used to tie an elephant to it.]

452. अतिदीर्घऽपि कर्णिकारी न मुसली।

No matter how big be an Okander tree, its wood can't be used to make a hammer. [Mere size can't ensure the quality of the contents.]

453- अति दीप्तोऽपि खद्योतो न पावक:।

Even excessive glowing can't turn a glow-worm into a fire-fling.

454- न प्रवृद्धत्व गुणहेतु:।

Excellence doesn't always give birth to good qualities. [An excellent player doesn't necessarily become a good man.]

455- सुजीर्णोऽपि पिचमुन्दो न शकुलायते।

No matter how old be a neem-tree, it cannot be used to make a nut-cutter. [Although neem-tree's wood is very strong which turns stronger with age, it can't become iron which is needed to make a nut-cutter!]

456. यथाबीजं तथा निष्पत्ति:।

One reaps as one sows. [If you plant a Babool tree, you can't get mango from it.]

457- यथा श्रव्तं तथा बुद्धि।

One's intelligence is conditioned by what one listens.

[Reared in an atmosphere resonating with abuses, you'll never chant holy shlokas.]

458. यथा कुलं तथाऽऽचार:।

One gets his character in accordance with his family traits.

459. संस्कृत पिचमन्दौ सहकारनवति।

No matter how much a neem-tree ripens, it can't turn into a mango tree.

460. न चागतं सुखं त्यजेत्।

Don't forego the available pleasure in the hope of enjoying a bigger one in future. [For no one can be sure of it in future as 'there are many a slip between the cup and the lip.']

461. स्वयमेव दु:खमधिगच्छति।

A man himself invites his misries.

462. रात्रि चारणं न कुयति।

Never wander aimlessly during night. [Gentle persons should not do so. It is the habit of rogues and whores.]

463. न चार्द्ध रात्रं स्व पेत।

Don't go to sleep at mid-night. [If one goes to sleep at mid-night, one may not get up at the day

break and this way one's whole schedule for the day will be disturbed.]

464. तद्विद्वदिम परीक्षेत।

Talk to the scholars for knowing about God.

465. पर गृहम् कारण न प्रविशेत्।

Don't enter other's house without any reason.

466. ज्ञात्वापि दोषमेव करोति लोक:।

People commit crimes knowingly.

467. शास्त्राप्रधना लोकवृत्ति:।

Social conduct is governed by the scriptural knowledge.

468. शास्त्राभावे शिष्टाचारमनुगच्छेत्।

Where scriptural dictates are absent, follow social manners/ customs.

469. ना चरिताच्छास्त्रां गरीय:।

Scriptures don't get precedence over social customs.

470. दूरस्थमपि चारचक्षुः पश्यति राजा।

Through his intelligence network, a king can seen (or examine) a thing lying far away.

471. गतानुगतिको लोको।

People behave after seeing other's behaviour. [People generally have a repeatative mentality. They love to follow blindly rather than think and chart out their course of action. But those who use their brain while observing other's behaviour generally get greater success in their endeavours.]

472. यमनुजीवेत्तं नापवदेत्।

Never criticize (or censure) the one on whose favour depends your survival or earning.

473. तपः सारः इन्द्रियनिग्रहः।

The essence of all penances is exercising control over your senses.

474. दुर्लभः स्त्रीबन्धनान्मोक्षः।

Redemption is an impossibility if one falls in the attraction of woman. [Chanakya repeats here an old classical belief of

India. Salvation is an impossibility if one falls in the clutches of a woman's charms.]

475- स्त्रीनामं सर्वाशुभानां क्षत्रम्।

[It is in continuation of the previous Sutra] For women are the root of all evils.

476. न च स्त्रीणां पुरुष परीक्षा।

A woman cannot judge the qualities of a man.

477- स्त्रीणां मनः क्षणिकम्।

Women are (generally) fickle minded.

478. अशुभ द्वेषिणः स्त्रीषु न प्रसक्ता।

Who remain away from bad habits never fall a prey to women.

479- यशपफलज्ञास्त्रिवेदविदः।

Those who are versed in the knowledge of the Vedas know the consequence of any yagya (sacrifice or action).

480. स्वर्गस्थानम् न शाश्वतम् यावत्पुण्य फलं।

One's position in heaven is not eternal. [One may get a place in heaven as the consequence of one's meritorious deeds yet, that position is not eternal. Because when that effect is over, one has to again come back to the mortal world.]

481. न च स्वर्ग पतनात्परं दुःखम।

Fall from heaven gives one extreme sorrow. [Hence one must keep on doing good deeds even if one has attained heaven. Only then one's stay in heaven can be prolonged. Otherwise one will have to fall from heaven which is a very painful experience.]

482. देही देहं त्यक्त्वा ऐन्द्रपदं न वाञ्छति।

A living being never wants to quit his body even if he is offered the Indra's position in heaven.

483. दुःखानामौषधं निर्वाणम्।

Final emancipation (Nirvana) is the panacea of all worldly miseries.

484. अनार्यसम्बन्धाद् वरमार्यशत्रुता।

A wise enemy is better than a foolish friend.

485. निहन्ति दुर्वचनं कुलम्।

Harsh and unpleasant words can even destroy families.

486. न पुत्रसंस्पर्शात्परं सुखम्।

No happiness is greater than caressing one's own son.

487. विवादे धर्ममनुस्मरेत्।

In no discussion or altercation should one forget one's religious dictates.

488. निशान्ते कार्यं चिन्तयेत्।

Plan your course of action at the end of the night (that is at dawn). [Because at dawn your mind will be fresh and alert.]

489. प्रदोषे न संयोगः कर्तव्यः।

Don't indulge in sex at the day break (with your wife).

490. उपस्थित विनाशो दुर्नयं मन्यते।

Facing the doom one resorts to unjust measures.

491. क्षीरार्थिनः किं करिष्यः।

What will a man, desiring milk, do with a female elephant? [He would like to have a cow or buffalo which can give him milk he likes. The comparison between a female elephant and a cow highlights the fact that a huge elephant will be of no use when one desires a tiny milk of cow.]

492. न दानसमं वश्यं वश्यम।

There is no favour/obligation like indulging in charity.

493. पराय त्तेषूत्कण्ठा न कुर्यात्।

Never desire impatiently for a thing gone in other's possession.

494. असत्समृद्धिरसद्भिरेव भुज्येत।

Ill-earned money gets consumed in the ill-company.

495. निम्बपफलं काकैरेव भुज्यते।

The (bitter) neem-fruit is eaten only by crows (bad persons).

496. नाम्भोधिस्तृष्णामपोहति।

Sea-water cannot quench the thirst.

497. बालुका अपि स्वगुण माश्रयन्ते।

Sand also follows its defined conduct. [Even the most useless thing like sand has its own way of showing its behaviour. Thus, even most insignificant man has his own life.]

498. सन्तोऽसत्सु न रमन्ते।

The saintly persons never enjoy the company of the rogues.

499. न हंसः प्रेतवने रमन्ते।

(Like) A swan can't enjoy in a cremation ground.

500. अर्थाथ प्रवर्तते लोकः।

The world works for serving its financial gains (or money). [The entire world has one driving force for work – money.]

501. आशया बध्यते लोकः।

Hope holds the world together. [It is hope which links everybody to the world and this way world remains a world.]

502. न चाशापरेः श्री सह तिष्ठति।

Wealth does not stay with a man who only hopes but doesn't make efforts to get it.

503. आशापरे न धैर्यम्।

One can't be patient if he hopes all the time. [Those who

only hope but don't make any effort to fulfill it, are prone to ever growing impatience.]

504. दैन्यान्मरणमुत्तमम्।

Death is better than suffering poverty.

505. आशा लज्जां व्यपोहति।

Those who keep on hoping (callously) only are devoid of shame. [They have no inhibition].

506. नमाता सह वासः कर्त्तव्यः।

A son should not stay alone with even his mother.

507. आत्मा न स्तोत्वयः।

One should not praise one's own self. ['Self-praise is no recommendation' – the same thought is emphasized here.]

508. न दिवा स्वप्नं कुर्यात्।

No one should sleep during day time. [Day time is meant for working. Only the callous, lethargic, work-shirkers sleep during day time.]

509. न चासन्नमपि पश्येत्यैश्वर्यान्ध न ऋणोतीष्टं वाक्यम्।

A man blinded by the lust of money doesn't listen to sane advice.

510. स्त्रीणां न भर्तुः परंदैवतम्।

No deity is greater than her husband for a woman.

511. तदनुवर्तनमुभयसुखम्।

Both (husband and wife) must act accordingly if they want happiness. [It is in continuation with the previous Sutra. Which the husband should be the ultimate God for a women, the husband also deem his wife as a unique gift of God. If they live with this relationship they will always be happy.]

512. अतिथिमभ्यागतं पूजये यथाविधिः।

Give as much respect to a guest at your home as much is possible. [It is highlighting the old Indian belief that a guest is a God and should be adored with all possible means.]

513. नास्ति हव्यस्य व्याघातः।

No noble act [whether offering made at a sacrifice for a noble cause or even education imparted to a deserving disciple] goes waste and unrewarded.

514. शत्रुर्मित्रवत् प्रतिभाति।

An enemy appears like a friend when your wisdom or vision is clouded.

515. मृगतृष्णा जलवत् भाति।

(Then) The sand of a desert may appear like waving water (when the vision is clouded).

516. दुर्मेध्सामसच्छास्त्रं मोहयति।

The fools love the books giving untrue advice. [The fools are tempted to read those books that are full of untruth.]

517. सत्संग: स्वर्गवास:।

The company of the pious/noble men (Saints) makes one dwell in heaven.

518. आर्य: स्वमिव परं मन्यते।

The noblemen consider others as equal with themselves. [That is, the noblemen do not treat anyone inferior or superior to them. They treat all as equal.]

519. रूपानुवर्ती गुण:।

Good qualities reflect on one's physical appearance. [Face is one's heart's mirror. Good or bad qualities reflect on one's face.]

520. यत्र सुखेन वर्तते देव स्थानम्।

Good place is that where one gets happiness.

521. विश्वासघातिनो न निष्कृतिः।

A treacherous person never gets liberated (from his or her guilty conscience).

522. दैवायत्तं न शोचयेत।

One shouldn't sorrow on his misfortune.

523. आश्रित दुःखमात्मन इव मन्यते साधुः।

The noble men deem their dependent's problems as their very own.

524. हृद्गतमाच्छाद्यान्यद् वदत्यनार्यः।

The mean hide their true emotions and never reveal their true feelings.

525. बुद्धिहीनः पिशाच तुल्य।

A man sans intelligence is like a wretch.

526. असहायः पथि न गच्छेत्।

Never go on a way you get no support. [One should never take a way where one may get no help or support.]

527. पुत्रे न स्तोतव्यः।

One should never praise his son on face. [For such a praise may turn him complacent and arrogant].

528. स्वामी स्तोतव्योऽनुजीविभिः।

(But) The servants should always praise their master.

529. धर्मकृत्येष्वपि स्वामिन वं घोषयेत्।

The servants should give sole credit to their masters under whose instructions they perform theholy rituals.

530. राजाज्ञां नातिलंघेत्।

The royal order should never be violated.

531. यथाऽऽज्ञप्तं तथा कुर्यात्।

It (the royal order) should be obeyed devotedly .

532. नास्ति बुद्धिमतां शत्रुः।

The wise have no enemies.

533. आत्मछिद्रं न प्रकाशयेत्।

Never reveal your weakness before anyone.

534. क्षमानेव सर्व साध्यति।

A forgiving person gets praise from all.

535. आपदर्थ धनं रक्षेत।

Save money to protect yourself from distress.

536. साहसवतां प्रियं कर्त्तव्यम।

Work is dear to daring person.

537. श्व कार्यमद्य कुर्वीत्।

Do tomorrow's work to-day only. [Don't postpone your work.]

538. आपराह्णिकं पूर्वाहत एवं कर्त्तव्यम्।

[Try to] Complete the afternoon's work in the morning itself.

539. व्यवहारानुलोभो धर्मः।

Acting in conformity to one's social norms is tantamount to adhering to one's religious faith. [For Chanakya always maintained that the social norms and the religious dictates always concur.]

540. सर्वज्ञता लोकज्ञता।

One who knows the world knows all.

541. शास्त्रोऽपि लोकज्ञो मूर्ख तुल्यः।

One who has the scriptural knowledge but no worldly knowledge is like a fool. [Again the fact is being emphasized that the scriptural dictates and social norms must concur.]

542. शास्त्र प्रयोजनं तत्त्व दर्शनम्।

[For] The purpose of the scriptural knowledge is to find the actual knowledge of all things.

543. तत्त्वज्ञानं कार्यमेव प्रकाशयति।

Work enlightens one about the real knowledge.

544- व्यवहारे पक्षपाते न कार्यः।

Never have a discriminatory behaviour.

545- धर्मादपि व्यवहारो गरीयान्।

[For] One's social conduct is more important than one's religious faith.

546- आत्मा हि व्यवहारस्य साक्षी।

One's soul is the [sole] witness of one's conduct.

547- सर्वसाक्षी ह्यात्मा।

One's soul is the universal witness. [One can't hide his own action from his soul. It is present everywhere.]

548- न स्यात् कूटसाक्षी।

[Therefore] Never be a false witness.

549- कूटसाक्षिणो नरके पतन्ति।

[Those who appear as] The false witness goes to hell.

550. प्रच्छन्नपापानां साक्षिणो महाभूतानि।

The five elements also witness the hidden acts of sin.

551. आत्मनः पापमात्मैव प्रकाशयति।

One's soul always reveals to his own acts of sin. [That is, one can't hide his sin from his soul.]

552. व्यवहारेऽन्तर्गतमाचारः सूचयति।

One's character is identified by his behaviour.

553. आकारसंवरणं देवानामशक्यम्।

Human behaviour is reflected by his face. Even the deities can't hide it.

554. चोर राजपुरुषेभ्यो दित्तं रक्षते।

Save your wealth from the royal-men and thieves. [The royal men or agents can always pounce upon you to take their share – due or undue. Hence they are as dangerous as thieves.]

555. दुर्दर्शना हि राजानः प्रजाः नाशयन्ति।

The king rarely seen often destroys his subjects. [Because

in accessibility to his presence deprives his subjects from conveying their grievances. Hence an indifferent king causes his people's downfall.]

556. सुदर्शना हि राजानः प्रजाः रञ्जयन्ति।

The king easily accessible to his subjects keeps them happy.

557. न्याययुक्तं राजानं मातरं मन्यते प्रजाः।

A just king is deemed like a mother by the subjects.

558. तादृशः स राजा इह सुखं ततः स्वर्गमाप्नोति।

Acting this way (as explained in the previous Sutra) such a king enjoys all pleasures of this world and gets heaven after his death.

559. अहिंसा लक्षणो धर्मः।

Non-violence is the basic tenet of every religious faith.

560.शरीरमणिए पर शरीरं मन्यते साधुः।

Holy men deem their body as though it is not their own. [Because they use it invariably for other's welfare.]

561. मांसभक्षणमयुक्तं सर्वेषाम्।

Eating meat (flesh) is bad for all.

562. न संसार भयं ज्ञानवताम्।

The wise persons are not afraid of the world. [Because they know that it is fey and transient.]

563. विज्ञान दीपेन संसार भयं निवर्तति।

[Because] The lamp of their scientific knowledge removes the fear of the world.

564. सर्वमनित्यं भवति।

Everything (in this fey world) is mortal.

565. कृमिशकृन्मूत्रभाजनं शरीरं पुण्यपपजन्महेतुः।

Because all sins and merits are committed by this body which essentially a store house of urine and faces, hence why must one has love for this body?

566. जन्मभरणादिषु दुःखमेव।

Sorrow is the end result of every birth and death.

567. सतेम्यस्तर्तु प्रयर्तत्।

beyond this birth-death cycle.

568. तपसा स्वर्गमाप्नोति।

Only penance (or holy deeds) can make one attain heaven.

569. क्षमायुक्तस्य तपो विवर्धते।

He who is forgiving by nature enhances the firmness in his penance.

570. सक्ष्मात् सर्वेषां कार्यसिद्धिर्भवति।

[With these measures] One achieves success in whatever he does. [Who is forgiving by nature, firm in his faith and committed to his penance eventually gets success in his every endeavour.]